# UNDESIRED AND DESIRED:

## CLIMATE CHANGE IN SOUTH ASIA

**Raghu Bir Bista, PhD**

January 2018

# UNDESIRED AND DESIRED:

# CLIMATE CHANGE IN SOUTH ASIA

(First Edition)

# UNDESIRED AND DESIRED:

## CLIMATE CHANGE IN SOUTH ASIA

(First Edition)

**Raghu Bir Bista, PhD**
**Associate Professor of Economics,**
**Tribhuvan University**

**CENTER FOR INTEGRATED DEVELOPMENT STUDIES**

**Lalitpur, Kathmandu**
**January 2018**

# UNDESIRED AND DESIRED:
## CLIMATE CHANGE IN SOUTH ASIA

Author: Raghu Bir Bista

Edition: First Edition, 2018



ISBN: 979-8679-5-0537-7

Publisher: Center for Integrated Development Studies, Lalitpur, Kathmandu and AMAZON

Distributor: AMAZON and New Hira Books Enterprises, Kathmandu, Phone: 01-4336618

Contact Email: cidsnepal2005@ yahoo.com

Author Email: bistanepal@gmail.com

In memory of climate change-induced disaster victims and vulnerable families during the undesired disaster all over the world, despite their innocence

# PREFACE

Climate change is an undesired but predicated threat in the World, particularly in Asia and Africa. In South Asia, its threat level is simultaneously well distributed with heterogeneity and homogeneity and its outcomes are never thought and expected in a wider spectrum. Despite cultural and historical bonds in South Asia, Nepal, Bhutan, and Pakistan have multiple natural hazards but Bangladesh, India, Maldives, and Sri Lanka have coastal floods, and cyclones, and water-induced disasters. For example the growth of glacier bursting, higher intensity, and frequency of floods in small streams and big streams, changing pattern of monsoon course and its intensity. About 100 million populations are found vulnerable from 700 events climate change and disaster after 1970.

In this context, this book is an output of academic research at Sotkhola water basin and its catchment areas in Surkhet, Karnali region ((at present located in the Province No 7) conducted in the last three years long (2014-2017) for my Ph.D. and updated in 2020. This study area was a hotspot of climate change study after the unexpected disastrous flooding of Sotkhola stream and landslides in its catchment areas in 2014 and found multiple natural hazards at grass root level as supplementary and complementary to climate change assessment at the national and regional level. Similarly, the climate change issue was assessed descriptively and exploratively and assessed forecasting method for climatic variable movements and trends for tracing its future in the next 30 years. Its scientific outputs might be relevant to the emerging underused growth of climate change threat level and the local household level vulnerability and adaptation behavior. However, I was undecided for a long time whether this scientific output should be published or not. I consulted my Professors and Researchers about it with my scientific outputs. Then, ultimately, I argued that if it was published, its output would contribute to the literature of climate change for further research, and scholars of climate change and adaptation would have positive outcomes to contribute and make clarity on climate change issues. As per theme and location, my scientific work was virgin and original that could open up a huge scope of research to understand the nitty-gritty of climate change and its dynamic dimension and its induced disaster events and effects.

This book focuses specifically only on climate change in that water basin and its catchment areas, national and regional level. I try to know and understand about climate change issues endorsed by the world, although the people of Nepal have been experiencing badly its attributes in terms of its events induced disastrous effects such as increasing snow melting, bursting glaciers, disturbance of monsoon cycle, fluctuating the rainfall patterns and intensity and attacks of mosquitoes in a cold place. The local people have their endogeneity in terms of knowledge, skill, perspectives, and behaviors on such undesired events for productive activity, livelihood, survival, and security. Based on facts, figures, and evidence, this book assesses climate change status, pattern and its undesired effects, the adaptative capacity of local people, and their behavior and exposure. Its outcomes will be valuable inputs to the society as well as the state mechanism for policy test and effectiveness for climate stability for our survival in next 2050.

November 23, 2019

Raghu Bir Bista, PhD

# ACKNOWLEDGEMENTS

Facts, figures, and evidence collected during the research on Climate Risks Assessment, Preparation of Integrated Watershed Management Plan and Assessment for CB-EWS for Sot-Khola Watershed, Surkhet, and data analysis and modeling during my Ph.D. work have made sufficient motivational and materialistic foundation to produce this book. In addition, my Professor Dr. Joy Shree Roy, Jadavpur University, Calcutta, and her course book, Stern's Review on Climate Change have contributed much more to see and understand in-depth facts, figures, and evidence of climatic variables and their behavior and the local people's responses and interaction. Thus, I would be able to make a broader horizon of knowledge on climate change and its effects and local people's adaptation behavior in this book format.

Book writing in social science is tough *good karma*. It is an outcome of genuine supports and contributions from its pre and post-process. I acknowledge all their supports and contributions and them with my honorable genuine gratitude.

I got an opportunity to discuss and go through its write-up and analysis with Professor Dr. Ram Prasad Gayanwaly and Professor Dr. Khet Raj Dahal for its pre manuscript phase. Associate Professor Dr. Ranjan Kumar Dahal had read its pre manuscript. He provided me valuable suggestions and technical and academic feedbacks, along with his moral, motivational and academic support. Dr. Manita Timilsina had looked at its GIS maps of the Sotkhola water sub-basin and its catchment areas and Nepal's map. Manoj Choudhary, office assistant for their administrative, information, and material support of Geo Tech had provided homely logistic support during my three nights stay in the office when Nepal was in Indian locked.

I am very thankful to Deepak K.C, Program Officer, UNDP for this collaboration work in Sot Khola Sub Water Basin and for the liberty to use the survey data for this work. I am very grateful to Budhi Sapkota, Former Chairman, and Bhim Sapkota, Executive Director, Sundar Nepal, Surkhet, for their accommodation, facilitation, guidance, and assistant for my household survey and carbon inventory. I would like to extend gratitude to surveyors Mr. Kul Deep Poudel, Mr. Kirti Sapkota, Dinesh Neupane, Uma G.C., and Dubita Sunar.

I would like to thank Sid Clouston, Clouston Energy Research, USA for their motivation, material, and suggestions to forward this book. I will extend my thanks to Prof. Joyshree Roy, Jadavpur University, Calcutta, Prof. Steve Forester, New University, USA, Prof, and President Douglass Capogrossi, Akamai University, USA, and Prof Mirjana Radovic, Belgrade.

Finally, I appreciate my family members for their lovely family support for making the required basic environment in the house. My special thanks go to my beloved wife Ramita Bista and my lovely mother Rajani Bista, along with the Bista family.

Raghu Bir Bista, PhD
November 2019

# CONTENTS


Preface
Acknowledge
List of Acronyms/ Abbreviation
List of Figures
List of Tables
Executive Summary

Chapter 1 : Introduction ..................................................................................................1

Chapter 2 : Overview of Climate Change ...........................................................20

Chapter 3 : Climate Change in South Asia ..........................................................51

Chapter 4 : Climate Change in Nepal ...................................................................86

Chapter 5 : Conclusion ...........................................................................................103

Reference

Annex

# ACRONYMS

| | |
|---|---|
| AC | Adaptive Capacity |
| AGDP | Agricultural Gross Domestic Product |
| AR4 | Fourth Assessment Report |
| AR5 | Fifth Assessment Report |
| BAU | Business as Usual |
| BCR | Benefit Cost Ratio |
| CBS | Central Bureau of Statistics |
| CBA | Cost Benefit Analysis |
| CC | Climate Change |
| C-D | Cobb Douglass (Production Function) |
| CGE | Computable General Equilibrium |
| CPI | The Consumer Price Index |
| CSI | Climate Sensitivity Indicators |
| CST | Committee on Science and Technology |
| CVI | Climate Vulnerability Index |
| DDC | District Development Committee |
| DF | Damaging Fluctuations |
| DHM | Department of Hydrology and Meteorology |
| EP | Expected Poverty |
| EEPSEA | the Economy and Environment Program for Southeast Asia |
| GDP | Gross Domestic Product |
| GIS | Geological Information System |
| GHG | Green House Gas |
| GLOF | Glacial Lake Outburst Floods |
| GOs | Government Organizations |
| GON | Government of Nepal |
| GPS | The Global Positioning System |
| HDI | Human Development Index |
| HH | Household |
| HVI | Household Vulnerability Index |
| IHE | Institute for Hydraulic and Environmental Engineering |
| IPCC | Inter-Governmental Panel on Climate Change |
| KG | Kilo Gram |
| LDC | Least Development Countries |
| MOAC | Ministry of Agriculture and Cooperatives |
| MPI | Market Performance Index |
| NARC | National Agricultural Research Center |
| NRB | National Rastriya Bank |
| NGOS | Non-Government Organizations |
| OECD | Organization of Economic Cooperation and Development |
| RMNP | Riding Mountain National Park |
| SAR | Second Assessment Report |
| SPSS | Statistical Pacakage for Social Science |
| TAR | Third Assessment Report |
| UNDP | United Nations Development Program |

| UNFCCC | United Nations Framework Convention on Climate Change |
| UNEP | United Nations Environment Program |
| USGCS | United States Green Cove Springs |
| UNESCO | The United Nations Organization for Education, Science and Culture |
| US | United States |
| USD | United States Dollar |
| VDC | Village Development Committee |
| VEP | Vulnerability Event Program |
| VEP | Vulnerability as Expected Poverty |
| VER | Vulnerability as uninured Exposure to Risk |
| VEU | Vulnerability Event Unit |
| VEU | Vulnerability as Expected Utility |
| VI | Vulnerability Index |
| WER | World Exposure Report |
| WHO | World Health Organization |
| WMO | World Metrological Organization |

# LIST OF FIGURES


Figure 1: Climate change in Asia................................................................38
Figure 2: Observed Climate Change in Asia .............................................43
Figure 3: Precipitation Distribution ..........................................................56
Figure 4: Mean Annual Temperature Trend line from 1980 to 2019 ..........59
Figure 5: Mean National Monthly Temperature of 1980 and 2017 .............61
Figure 6: Stationwise Mean National Temperature from 1980 to 2019 ..........62
Figure 7: Mean National Rainfall from 1980 to 2019....................................65
Figure 8: Mean National Rainfall from 1995 to 2019....................................67
Figure 9: Mean Rainfall Trend of Surkhet from 1995 to 2019 .....................70
Figure 10: Mean Rainfall by Month.............................................................73
Figure 11: Mean Temperature of Surkhet from 1980 to 2017.......................76
Figure 12: Monthly Temperature & Mean Temperature (1980-2017) ........77
Figure 13: Study Area (Sot Khola sub water basin and catchment area)..........107
Figure 14: Sot Khola Catchment Areas .....................................................108
Figure 15: Analytical Framework for Vulnerability Assessment ....................111
Figure 16: Indicator & Index Method..........................................................112


# LIST OF TABLES


Table 1: GHG Emission Reduction Target by 2020 .......................................29
Table 2: Weather Distribution and Climatic variables ....................................54
Table 3: Ecological Distribution and Status .................................................55
Table 4: Descriptive Statistics of Temperature and Rainfall from 1980 to 201956
Table 5: Descriptive Statistics of Annual Temperature across Stations .............57
Table 6: Economic & Human Loss from 2000 to 2018..................................66
Table 7: Climate change in local areas ........................................................78
Table 8: Ecological Elevation ....................................................................104
Table 9: Topography Distribution ..............................................................105
Table 10: Cluster Division and Distribution.................................................115

# EXECUTIVE SUMMARY

In the last 100 years, climate change issues have been bigger than in the past in the world as transboundary issues inclusively and exclusively, along with its wider economic losses and human losses. Its reflection can be found in developing countries like Nepal with GHG emissions and without GHG emissions. Similarly, Climate change in Nepal has become an important issue with experiencing a higher frequency of natural calamities, variability of rainfall, and mean temperature rising all over the country and its impacts in terms of damage and losses. Its vulnerability has been a complex and critical issue. In this context, this study has the overall objective: to measure climate change vulnerability and household behavior at the household level and community level in Nepal. Its specific objectives are: 1) to measure climate change vulnerability in the different parts of Nepal, 2) to construct climate change vulnerability index of the study area, 3) to identify factors influencing climate change vulnerability of households and its effects on the study area and 4) to analyze household's adaptation behavior undertaken at household and community level.

The study is based on primary cum secondary data sets as a required theoretical model of climate change vulnerability index to capture the household vulnerability and semi-log regression econometric models based on C-D production function for capturing household vulnerability and adaptation behavior. The primary data were collected from 642 random sample households through Household Survey in 2015 in three VDCs: Gadhi, Lekgaon, and Kunathari, and secondary data of temperature and rainfall were used from 1980 to 2019 from the Department of Hydrology and Meteorology, the Government of Nepal.

The study shows the variation in temperature and rainfall in Nepal due to heterogeneous altitudes. The highest altitude has the lowest temperature and the lowest altitude has the highest temperature. It shows the winter season is colder than before and summer is hotter than before. Thus, climate change in the different parts of Nepal occurs, like in the study area: Sot Khola Sub Water Basin, along with climatic disasters.

# Chapter One

# INTRODUCTION

Climate change has become an emerging undesired sensitive disaster issue in developing countries like Nepal. Large scientific evidence indicates a fact that the earth's climate system is rapidly changing as a result of increases in the concentration of Green House Gas (GHG) in the atmosphere caused by human activities (Stern, 2006).  To meet a thirst for higher economic growth, welfare, and prosperity, human activities-industrial development, agricultural production, transport development, housing, cutting trees, etc are blindly aggressive with competitive motives and feelings to harass non-renewable and renewable natural resources more and more in the cost of changing the earth's climate.  Its examples are deforestation and burning fossil fuels.  Its bad result is the growth of carbon dioxide ($CO_2$) from 344.3 ppm in 1984 to 405.5ppm in 2017 with 146 percent growth rate today, the growth of methane ($CH_4$) from 1653ppb in 1984 to 1859 ppb in 2017 with 257 percent change and the change of nitrogen oxide ($N_2O$) from 303.5ppb in 1984 to 329.9 ppb in 2017 with 122 percent growth. Such level of GHG emissions are caused by energy (21.3%), industry (16.8%), transport (14%), agriculture (12.5%), mineral processing (11.3%), housing (10.3%), land use/deforestation (10%) and waste (3.4%). Despite being its transboundary nature and character, the growth of GHG emission is dominantly contributed by developed countries for achieving higher economic growth and higher per capita income growth. In 2017, USA and USSR contributed 30 percent followed by China (8%) and then other countries with negligible percent. Its result was a 2.23 trillion USD economic loss between 1998 and 2017. USA had a 1 trillion USD economic loss followed by China, India, etc (UN, 2019). If it is not stabilized, the world will have a big threat with risk and loss.

Its appearing nature, pattern, trend, inducement, and risk in developing countries are not noticeable different from what Stern's Review (2006) projected about it. Its example is Asian countries. Stern (2007) estimated the projected $2^0C$-$3^0C$ temperature rise in the next 50 years. Eliasch (2008) verified this projection by explaining that more than half of the population has experienced the variation in the global temperature in the world by $0.7^0C$ over the past decades. IPCC (2001) considers capriciously such scientific results for mass dissemination and test. IPCC (2001) projects the Earth's mean surface temperature warm 1.4 to $5.8^0C$ by the end of the 21st century, with land areas warming more than the oceans and the high altitudes warming more than the tropics, with an increase in heavy precipitation events. It affects individual organisms, populations, species distributions, and ecosystem composition and function. Globally by the year 2080, about 20 percent of coastal wetlands could be lost due to sea-level rise

1mm-2mm on average per year. Snow cover in the northern hemisphere has decreased by 10 percent on average since the late 1960s. Further, the risk of extinction will increase for many species, which are already vulnerable. Few but vital national-level studies in Bangladesh, China, India, Thailand, Vietnam, and Nepal have validated such results. In next 2050, the population size will be 8.7 billion and will expand to 15 billion at the end of the century. It means 10-26 times more GDP growth simultaneously. Let us imagine such growth of population and GDP will consume how many resources and generate how much anthropogenic $CO_2$ to induce climate change and its disasters.

Climatic events such as melting glaciers, decreasing snow cover malfunction of the hydrological cycle, disturbance of monsoon cycle, flooding, drought and cyclones referring temperature rising have increasing trend, devasting nature, unpredicted pattern and undesired disaster inducement more than before in different national metrological database and reports. In addition, climate change has increased the risk level to the terrestrial and aquatic ecosystem, biodiversity, species, crops, etc towards extinction due to forest fire and land degradation. Of a total of 59 plants, 47 invertebrates, 29 amphibians and reptiles, 388 birds, and 10 mammal species, approximately 80 percent showed a change in the biological parameters (breeding seasons, migration patterns, distributions of animals and plants, and changing body size) but about 20 percent showed a change in the opposite direction (CBS, 2017). In the temperate and high-altitude areas, some ecosystems that is particularly sensitive to changes in the regional climate. The ranges of butterflies in Europe and North America have been found to shift poleward and up in elevation as the temperature has increased. In the World, Stern (2006) argued mitigation measures as a potential alternative measure to stabilize climate change and minimize climatic events. Otherwise, he projected a huge damage cost of GDP loss of developing countries higher than developed countries in the future (Stern, 2006). In Asia, human displacement was recorded by nearly 7 million people in India and 15 million people in Bangladesh (Nicholl, Leatherman, K.C. and Volonte, 1995). The 1993 flood disaster fully and partially affected nearly 28,000 families in the middle mountains and 42,000 families in the lowlands (Chalise and Khanal, 2002). Further, a large population of developing countries particularly African and Asian countries will suffer from malnutrition, food deficit, water scarcity, deaths, and diseases in the future (Stern, 2006). In the absence of adaptation measures to climate change, South Asia could lose an equivalent of 1.8% of its annual gross domestic product (GDP) by 2050 and 8.8% by 2100 (Ahmed and Suphachalasai 2014). The average total economic losses are projected to be 9.4% for Bangladesh, 6.6% for Bhutan, 8.7% for India, 12.6% for the

Maldives, 9.9% for Nepal, and 6.5% for Sri Lanka (Aryal, Khatri Cheetri, Khurana, and Sapkota, 2019). Thus, the growth of climate change and disaster-induced vulnerability has become a big potential threat in developing countries, particularly in Asia.

Like other developing countries in Asia, Nepal has been experiencing undesirably and badly a higher frequency of natural calamities events (landslide, drought, cyclones, heat wave, fire, cold wave, snow storm, heavy rainfall, and flooding) as integrity with the seasonal cycle, variability of rainfall and average temperature rising across heterogenous location, geography and altitude over all over the country than earlier (1970). Like rainfall, there is the variability of mean temperature from $0.4^0$C to $0.6^0$C over 50 years long time all over the country (CBS, 2011). Similarly, Glacial lake outburst floods (GLOF) have occurred, namely Dudh Khosi GLOF 1985, Tamakhosi GLOF 1991, and Dudh Khosi GLOF, 1998 (Mool, Bajaracharya and Joshi, 2001a). The resulting flood wave destroyed the Namche hydropower plant and many bridges, along with the loss of valuable life. In addition, the higher intensity of rainfall over 48 hours induced floods have occurred in Nakhu Khola in 1981, Bagmati and Narayani in 1993, Andhi Khola in 1998, and Bagmati in 2002 (Chalise and Khanal, 2002). The 1991 flood not only destroyed nearly all the agricultural land in Le Le VDC, more than 48 houses and seven water turbines and but also killed twenty-seven people. The 1993 flood disaster fully and partially affected nearly 28,000 families in the middle mountains and 42,000 families in the lowlands (Chalise and Khanal, 2002). About 1000 people were killed during that climatic event. The 1996 Larcha debris flow washed away physical infrastructure including roads, bridges, and transmission lines, along with 18 houses. Floods of a smaller scale of less disastrous, but still considerable, impact occur annually to many locations (Chalise and Khanal, 2002). In addition, over 45 years (1971-2015), landslides killed 4832 people and destroyed 32819 houses. The fire killed 1541 people and damaged fully 83527 houses. Flood killed 4344 people and destructed 0.21 million houses (CBS, 2017). In the case of glacier bursting threats, glacier lakes are accounted for 2323 out of which about 15 glacier lakes were busted and about 12 glacier lakes are critical situation (CBS, 2017). Thus, climate change and disaster-induced higher vulnerability have made Nepal climate change prone country having 4th rank in the world climate change risk rank and 20th rank in the world multiple natural hazardous having a life-threatening in the course of overall development, social security, and human welfare.

It is a fact that climate change and disaster-induced vulnerability have uncalculated visible and invisible adverse effects directly and indirectly on a household's income, livelihood security, and welfare at the micro-level. In Nepal, its mean loss per annum was 27000 million Nepali Rupees (270 million USD (1$=100NPR) in 2013 price rate) including dead, missing, damage, loss of asset, death of livestock (CBS, 2011 and CBS, 2017). Despite its tiny loss size at the macro-level (i.e.0.6 %- 2 percent loss GDP ratio) without all indirect cost (GON, 2014), this worth of direct economic loss reduces household's income, livelihood security, and welfare and further expanding vertically and horizontally the poorest of the poor and extremity of the inequality level vertically between the 20 percent top income group and the 20 percent bottom income group. So far concerned with the poor and marginal households including small farmers and landless farmers, such disaster may make complicated deepening their poverty and inequality more than before. Thus, poverty reduction efforts at the micro level may be an ineffective policy matter, which needs a special package of fiscal recovery shock to correct policy transformation and delivery, along with dynamic, effective, and efficient local institution and their mechanisms during the policy implementation.

However, a large number of literature (Nicholls, Leatherman, K.C and Volonte, 1995; IPCC, 2001; Fussel and Kelin, 2003; Adger, 2006, Stern, 2006; Elisch, 2008 and UNFCCC, 2008) argue adaptation as the best short-term measure to improve household and community adaptive capacity to minimize such uncalculated and undesired severe vulnerability at some extent to save lives and assets. It is a fact that the household has such indigenous adaptive capacity in terms of knowledge and technology (Stern, 2006). Such property that seems to be innocently simple and has no meaning in the modern advanced society is invisibly available at household and community due to the knowledge transformation to new generation from the old generation through out disaster management process. In 1993, the Bagmati River flooded with heavy rainfall above the hills of Le Le. In Le le, about 65 years old person who listened swing sound of flooded Bagmati came out first and then rang a small bell. The sound was an alert of danger, a so-called indigenous early warning system. Then, the people came out with sleepy eyes to move to safe areas, along with their children and old age people (Le le, 1993). Similarly, the Sot Khola flood in 2014 was at nighttime. Rakshin village was in the lower and plain land but the river was far away from the village. Its depth was approximately 5 feet below the banks. Nobody imagines and thinks such height of water level. At midnight, the village was silently relaxing their body with a beautiful dream. An old villager when opened his eye to come in the toilet saw the river smoothly entered with the increasing water level. The old villager used a plate for ringing a bell alerting about such danger (Field Survey,

2015).   The plate was a small thing. However, his indigenous knowledge made it a big instrument for alerting and saving the life, and then villagers used trees for their safety urgently and waited for the silence of the floods natural roaring fearful music and most moved to somewhere top and safe places.

From time to time, households explicitly and confidently demonstrate adaptation behaviors to minimize climate change vulnerability either at the individual level or community level (Fussel, 2007). At the micro-level, the individual household has shown adaptation behavior to minimize the risk of death and loss of income, assets, and livestock.  In the Sotkhola flooding in 2014, all community in the catchment areas was just owl watching the water level and flooding during the whole night. Their collection of information and monitoring of the flood was adaptation behavior.  In addition, there was the use of fire for alerting.  In Bangladesh, about a million of populations migrated to the city for saving their life. So far, the possibility of huge damage, the household has escaped away (or seasonal or permanent migration) from that location. This migratory behavior of households can save life and asset (Adger, 2006).  In case of the loss of income, households have shown the behavior of changing crops and use of fertilizer. At the community level, the household has shown a long-term adaptation behavior as the intervention in irrigation development, forest conservation, and technology adaptation (Nicholls, Leatherman, K.C and Volonte, 1995). Thus, some sort of indigenous adaptive capacity reduces the severity of climate change and disaster-induced vulnerability. Like developing countries, Nepal's poor adaptation capacity has been a driver to make more complex and critical to climate change and disaster-induced vulnerability at mico and macro levels.

In Nepal, climate change has been happening in a different form, pattern, and event all over the country over a long time. When we talked with the local people about the temperature rising in the study area, they told their experience with increasing warming at summer and winter season and further explained summer was hotter than before and winter was less cold than before. It is an example of a qualitative measure of climate change. CBS (2017) shows about 56.79 percent urban population and 46.24 percent rural population having awareness of climate change. Similarly, males (54.07%) have more knowledge than females (39.08%). However, there is no quantitative measurement of temperature rising at the community level. Scientific studies, despite its handfuls, have serious efforts to quantify it based on scientific climatic data of metrology all over the country. In 2008, Malla (2008) quantified a $1.8^0$ C average temperature rise from 1975 to 2006 but Karn (2014) mentioned a $1^0$ C rise of mean temperature, which is higher than the global average. Whatever the difference in mean temperature rising, it is a fact of temperature rising over 30 years historical database. Malla (2008) further explained its disasters (frequent drought, severe floods, and landslides). Both scientific studies argue its negative impact on paddy yield, along with wheat and maize yield. GON (2014) presented a similar observation with a broader sense and in-depth coverage on climate change focusing more on adaptation and mitigation approach for its stability at the national level and local level.

In the case of climate change, western Nepal does not differ from national climate change reference and its induced disaster events. Acharya (2012) argued rising temperature with $2^0$C average per annum in western Nepal. However, it is relatively three times higher than the lower temperature within the country and significantly higher in the comparison of the global trend of temperature variation. His claim is a question of reliability and validity because of technical error. Over the last 36 years (1975-2010), the average temperature growth in western Nepal is 1.2° C, which is two times high of the global average. Bhandari (2013) supplements it by noting high temperature and low rainfall with its adverse effect of changing climate variables (high temperature and low rainfall) in Dedeldhura, western Nepal. The above literature indicates climate change in western Nepal with a temperature rising and rainfall decreasing.

Climate change induces disasters (landslides, floods, droughts, etc.). Dahal, Hasegawa, Nonomura, Yamanaka, Dhakal, and Paudyal (2008) established the proper relationship between rainfall and landslide. Karki, Shrestha, and Winiger (2011) linked it with flood and its hazard. Its socio-economic effects on the household in the country supplement it. Pant (2011) and Acharya and Bhatta (2013) have explained the negative impact of climate change in agriculture. Pant (2012) found a negative effect on the national self-sufficiency of food grains. Thus, climate change in western Nepal has become an emerging dangerous threat to human activity and livelihood in the next 50 years and at the end of this century too.

In western Nepal, the Sot Khola water basin (Figure 2) was notable water-related multi natural hazards diasters: flooding and landslides at the lower stream of the catchment areas with heavy erratic rainfall at the upper stream of the catchment areas in 2014 (DDC, 2015). In 2014, the Sot Khola stream was aggressively flooding from the upstream (Gadhi) to the downstream (Kunathari). In Gadhi and Lekhagaon, the flood was cutting heavily the cultivated land, trees, and small bushes on both sides of the stream and curbing road, clean drinking water, canals, bridges, pipelines, and houses from Gadhi to Lekhagaon and Kunathari VDC. In many low lands of Kunathari VDC, the flood was loading and dispositing of sedimentation of stones, sands, mud, trees, plants, small pieces of wood, etc in the cultivated land (Field Survey, 2015). As result, loading heavy sedimentation in the cultivated land degraded fertile soil and organic nutrition soil ingredients, and cutting the cultivated land banks reduced land size in the catchment areas. If sedimentation and cutting cultivated land were not maintained on time with the proper method, its adverse effect would be unexpectedly lower agricultural productivity and production against the higher cost of crop cultivation. Similarly, the loss of infrastructure and assets would make it critical to human livelihood and survival in the catchment areas (Field Survey, 2015). Similarly, the heavy rainfall-induced simultaneously dangerous numerous landslides and debris damaging ecological and geological structures, loading huge sedimentation in agricultural land and curbing crop, livestock, and houses in Gadhi, Lekhagaon, and Kunathari. Still, about 20 houses were critically exposed to landslides occurring above houses at 50 meters far from the house. If debris with sedimentation in agricultural land was not properly cleared on time with the proper method, its adverse would be lower productivity and production at the higher cost of crop cultivation and harvesting. Most had not maintained their land. Thus, residents lost directly and indirectly from crop and livestock loss. In the catchment areas, all residents had 66 percent losses in crop and 34 percent livestock losses. Its loss value was about Rs. 18,464,427 (18.4 million rupees) (0.18 million USD at (1 USD=100 rupees). Still, the catchment areas are economically and socially vulnerable areas with a higher risk of water-borne diseases and food insecurity to human life and livelihood. About 69 percent of households were vulnerable. Such multi-hazard had a huge cost of more than 30 million Rupees (DDC, 2015). Its result was increasing inequality and poverty levels at the catchment areas. Thus, climate change vulnerability has become a hazardous issue in the Sot Khola water basin and its catchment areas. This issue has generated serious attention and curiosity about what level of climate change vulnerability occurs in the different catchment areas of Sot Khola water basin, Surkhet, what are the adaptation capacity levels of households across different income and regions, and how much these adaptation behaviors either at individual or community level are effective. However, there is none of the literature studying climate change vulnerability and adaptive behavior in the Sot Khola water basin and its catchment areas, despite its critical vulnerability. Therefore, this study is relevant.

In this context, this book covers whether climate change vulnerability has higher intensity and huge cost, whether households across different income levels and regions have adaptation capacity, whether households' adaptation behaviors are effective to minimize climate change vulnerability. Its outcomes would be valuable information and data to the policy makers of Nepal to generate climate change vulnerability index and data information for specific noticeable mapping for initiating adaptation and mitigation policy and program intervention. Similarly, it would be valuable information on understanding the adaptation capacity of the household for developing adaptative capacity enhancement strategies and programs for improving the household's adaptation capacity and effective behavior. In the case of agriculture, it would be a good information source for irrigation and forest conservation program.

## OBJECTIVES OF THE BOOK

The overall objective of this book is to measure climate change: Status, Trend, and Forecasting in South Asia and Nepal.

## DATA AND METHODS

The book is based on a study on climate change in South Asia. Its research design was descriptive and explorative based on qualitative and quantitative data and information collected from primary and secondary sources of South Asia. The time-series data sets (1995-2018) were employed. Its analytical methods were descriptive tools and the time series forecasting model.

## ABOUT THE BOOK

The chapter scheme for this book is specifically divided into five chapters. They are as follows: Chapter I: Introduction, Chapter II: Overview of Climate Change, Chapter III: Climate Change in South Asia Chapter IV: Climate Change in Nepal, Chapter V: Conclusion.

Chapter I introduces the issues of the book along with motivation, aim and scope, contribution and relevancy, limitation, and chapter scheme. This chapter establishes climate change and its vulnerability in Nepal. In chapter II, the book develops its concept, dimensions, and evolution, along with climate change vulnerability and adaption. Then, the book includes climate change in Nepal in chapter III, analyzing climatic variables (rainfall and temperature rising) in South Asia and Nepal over the last 40 years metrological and hydrological time-series database with time series trend analysis and forecasting method. Naturally, its impacts follow severely presented in Chapter IV. Lastly, the book synthesis the conclusion of all chapters to explore empirical results conclusion, and lessons for a way forward to contribute to climate change stability and climate change vulnerability reduction, along with alternatives.

# Chapter Two
# CLIMATE CHANGE

This chapter reviews the evolution of climate change issues and the concept of climate change from the synthesis reviews of the relevant theoretical and empirical literature. This chapter mainly covers climate change.

## EXPLORATION AND EXPEDITION OF CLIMATE CHANGE ISSUE

No doubt, climate change has become a current emerging top most sensitive burning international issue as Tran's boundary issue with the future unpredictable unpleasant threats. We believe what we see, what we learn, and what we have. We do not believe what we do not see, what we do not learn, and what we have not. Reality is a bitter truth in which what we do not see, what we do not learn and what we have not. Similarly, this issue was a fact in history but was not learned. It got big attention on the changing the earth's climate, when the book, *the Limits to Growth* published in 1972 had raised a query about the sustainability of the Earth. The book analyzed twelve growth scenarios of global development over 200 years from 1900 to 2100 through the first use of the World Prediction Model. The book warned if the world population and industrial investment continue to increase, the resources will deplete, the environment will deteriorate and humankind will reach the limits of growth within 100 years (Behrens, Randers, Meadows and Meadow, 1972). Then, the international community realized strongly such scientific output, climate change issue as a big natural hazard and its disasters vulnerable outcomes at that time.

After 11 years of scientific discourse on climate change issue, the United Nations(UN) seriously responded through the formation of the Brundtland Commission in 1983 to re-examine such critical issues of environment and development and to formulate innovative, concrete, and realistic actions, to strengthen international cooperation on environment and development by finding new forms of cooperative models and to raise the level of understanding and commitment to action. Its key concern was to save the human environment and natural resources and prevent deterioration of economic and social development.

As follow up and concurrently scientific research, ozone layer research led a foundation stone of ratifying the Montreal Protocol (MP) in 1987. The protocol that relates to phasing out substances depleting the Ozone Layer is called a protocol to the Vienna Convention for the Protection of the Ozone Layer. It was the first mitigative initiation of the international community towards stabilizing climate change. Immediately after, in 1987, the Brutland Commission that is the World Commission on Environment and Development reported to the United Nations, and later the report was published as Our Common Future.  By its three key mandates: reexamine the critical issues of environment and development and formulate action proposals, find alternatives to develop international cooperation, and increase the level of understanding and commitment to action, the report identified poverty reduction, gender equity, and wealth redistribution as crucial to environmental conservation. It identified the environmental limits to economic growth in industrialized and industrializing societies and poverty as limiters and pressure to sustainability. It emphasizes the balance between economy and ecology by arguing the need for sustainable development. Further, it explains sustainable development as development that meets the needs of the present without compromising the ability of future generations to meet their own needs, although the report has not mentioned any alternative modes of production. Thus, it led the World towards sustainable development for our common future.

After five years, the World showed its strong perception, concern, and sensitivity on this issue with its request to establish an institution set up as a scientific intergovernmental body within the UN focusing on this issue. In 1988, the UN accepted such a request and established the Intergovernmental Panel on Climate Change (IPCC) in the framework of UNFCCC (United Nations Framework Convention on Climate Change), along with UNEP and World Metrological Organization (WMO). Thus, the UNFCCC framework has an objective of stabilization of Green House Gas (GHG) in the atmosphere to stabilize this Tran's boundary issue. Thus, the international community started collectively to respond to such critical issues.

The IPCC assessed comprehensively climate change and its thematic issues. In 1990, the IPCC published a first assessment report. IPCC (1990) mentioned that human-induced emissions increased substantially GHG concentration on the atmosphere and further global mean temperature would increase by to $0.3^0$ C per decade of business as usual (BAU). It concluded increasing $0.3^0$ C to $0.6^0$ C global mean surface air temperatures over the last 100 years.

In 1992, its supplement report followed with the conclusion of no effect on our fundamental understanding of the science of GHG. Simultaneously, the United Nations Conference on Environment and Development was held in Rio de Janeiro, Brazil in 1992 advocating the need for sustainable development comprehensively. It kept the foundation of the Kyoto Protocol. In the same year, the Framework Convention on Climate Change (UNFCCC) was endorsed to make Industrialized and industrializing countries for their strong commitment to reducing emissions to stabilize climate change.

The IPCC released a second assessment report (SAR) in 1995. IPCC (1995) concluded increasing GHG concentration due to man-made and natural and temperature rising between $0.3^0$ C and $0.6^0$ C since the 19th century. Despite uncertainties, there is the expectation of continuing to change temperature.

After two and half year's intense negotiations process, the international community reached to agree on the Kyoto Protocol at the third conference of the parties to the UNFCCC(COP3) in Kyoto, Japan on December 11, 1997. The protocol aims to fight against global warming based on emission reduction and emission reduction trading. Its basic binding is to achieve the quantified emission limitation and reduction commitments (mentioned in Article 2, Article 3, and Annex I). Mandatories to each Party are enhancement of energy efficiency in relevant sectors of the national economy; protection and enhancement of sinks and reservoirs of GHG not controlled by Montreal Protocol, taking into account its commitments under relevant international environmental agreements, promotion of sustainable forest management practices, afforestation and reforestation; promotion of sustainable form of agriculture in the light of climate change considerations; research on and promotion, development and increased use of, new and renewable forms of energy, of $CO_2$ sequestration technologies and of advanced and innovative environmentally  sound technologies; progressive reduction or phasing out of market imperfections, fiscal incentives, tax and duty exemptions and subsidies in all GHG emitting sectors that run counter to the objective of the convention and application of market instruments; encouragement of appropriate reforms in relevant  sectors aimed at promoting policies and measures which limit or reduce  emissions of GHGs not controlled by the Montreal Protocol; measures to limit and/or reduce emissions of GHG not controlled by the Montreal Protocol in Transport sector and Limitation and /or reduction of methane emissions through recovery and use in waster management, as well as in the production, transport and distribution of Energy.

The protocol has legally bonded to industrialized and industrializing countries to be responsible for bearing the cost for common interest based on emission.  It is a big burden to industrialized and industrializing countries to cut down emissions or to trade credit for constant emission. It proposed three innovative, concrete, and realistic mechanisms at minimum cost: Emission Trading, Joint Implementation, and Clean Development Mechanism (CDM).

The third assessment report (TAR) published in 2001 noted that the projected climate change would have negative impacts on both environmental and socio-economic systems but the larger changes and the rate of climate change. Further, the report identified vulnerable ecosystems and species. Mitigation and adaptation could lessen GHG pressure and the effect of climate change (IPCC, 2001). In 2002, the World Summit on Sustainable Development happened in Johannesburg.

Similarly, IPCC published a fourth assessment report (AR4) in 2007. IPCC (2007) explained increasing climate change impacts as growing frequencies and concentration of some extreme weather events, experience in rising warming and sea level, despite business as action, available of mitigation and adaptation activity.

Bali Action Plan (COP-13) that was endorsed in the 13th Conference of the Parties of the UNFCCC held in Bali, Indonesia in 2007 launched a comprehensive long cooperative process and action to implement the convention. Its central themes on negotiation were four including mitigation, adaptation, technology, and financing towards long-term emission reduction for climate change stability.

In 2012, Copenhagen Summit (COP15) was held. It aimed to reach a binding agreement in the post of Kyoto Protocol after 2012. At the summit, there were two parties' countries: the United States and the basic countries (China, India, South Africa, and Brazil) preparing the Copenhagen Accord to continue the Kyoto Protocol. The Accord continues climate change as one of the greatest challenges by emphasizing urgent combat climate change in the accordance with the principle of commons and differentiated responsibilities and respective capabilities to keep global temperature below $2^0$ C in the context of sustainable development. Secondly, it considers the need for a comprehensive adaptation program at the international level to minimize the critical impacts of climate change and the potential impacts of response measures in countries. Thirdly, it recognizes the need for deep cuts in global emissions according to the IPCC AR4 report by focusing international cooperation on global and national GHG reduction and low emission development strategy. Fourthly, it emphasizes the urgent need for enhanced action and international cooperation on adaptation to reduce vulnerability and build resilience in developing countries, particularly vulnerable countries, LDCs, SIDs, and Africa. It binds developed countries to provide adequate, predictable, and sustainable financial resources, technology, and capacity building to support the implementation of adaptation action in developing countries.

The Accord has emphasized the urgent need for mitigation. In Annex I of the Accord, the parties are bonded to commit to economy-wide emissions targets for 2020 and to agree to strengthen the implementation of the Kyoto Protocol and their targets. In addition, the Accord has the following agreements related to emission mitigation below. Firstly, developing countries agree to implement mitigation actions NAMA (Nationally

Appropriate Mitigation Actions) to slow growth in their CO2 emissions. LDC and SIDS agree to voluntarily action in this regard based on international support. Secondly, developing countries agree to report these actions once every two years. Thirdly, the Accord recognizes the crucial role of reducing emissions from deforestation and land degradation and the need to reduce GHG emission by forestation and $CO_2$ credit trading REDD-plus mechanism. Fourthly, the market will be an opportunity to enhance the cost-effectiveness measure to promote mitigation actions and to provide incentives to continue to develop low emission pathways adopted by developing countries. Fifthly, developed countries agreed to raise funds of $30 billion from 2010-2012 of new and additional resources and to raise $100 billion per year by 2020 from a wide variety of resources to help developing countries cut CO2 emissions. Sixthly, the Accord establishes a Copenhagen Green Climate Fund to support projects, programs, policies, and other activities in developing countries related to mitigation and establishes a Technology Mechanism to accelerate technology development and transfer. Seventhly, the Accord has a target to limit temperature rises to $1.5^0C$ in long term.

**Table 1: GHG Emission Reduction Target by 2020**

| Country | Target (%) | Country | Target (%) |
|---|---|---|---|
| Australia | 5.0-25 | Japan | 25 |
| Brazil | 36.1 | Mexico | 30 |
| Canada | 17 | Russia | 15 -25 |
| China | 40 -45 | South Africa | 34 |
| India | 20 - 25 | South Korea | 30 |
| Indonesia | 26 | United States | 17 |
| Israel | 20 | | |

Source: *UNFCCC, 2012*

In the Accord, the countries have committed to reducing GHG emissions by 2020 above table, although the first initial deadline of the Copenhagen Accord to about 80 percent global emitter countries was January 31, 2010(Table 1). Thus, the international community has adopted a mitigation approach to cut down GHG emissions to make BAU.

In 2010, the United Nations Climate Change Conference was held in Cancun, Mexico. Therefore, it was called the Cancun Summit (COP 16) in which four preparatory rounds of negotiations happened. It forwarded Kyoto Protocol Accord and Copenhagen Accord to achieve GHGs emission reduction and adaptation capacity of developing countries to reduce climate impacts and to achieve sustainable development.

The Cancun Summit had the following objectives as follows: to establish clear goals and schedule to reduce human-induced GHGs over time to keep the global average temperature rise below 20⁰C; to encourage the participation of all countries in reducing these emissions; review climate change action progress made towards 20C objective and review by 2015; to build low carbon society, to call the industrialized and industrializing countries to reduce GHGs as pledged in the Copenhagen Accord, along with developing countries; to develop and transfer clean technology to boost efforts to address climate change;  to mobilize and provide scale-up  funds in the short and long term to enable developing countries to take greater and effective action;  to set up the Green Climate Fund of $100 billion per year by 2020 to developing countries; to assist the particularly vulnerable people in the world to adapt to the inevitable impacts of climate change by taking  a coordinated approach to adaptation; to protect the World's forests; to build up global capacity and to establish effective institutions and systems.

The Cancun summits have reached the following Accords below: to establish the Cancun Adaptation Framework and the Adaptation Committee at regional and national level; to submit annual GHG inventories and inventory reports and biennial report on their action progress; to adopt nationally appropriate mitigation actions(NAMA) to BAU emissions by 2020; to set up a registry to record NAMA seeking international support and to facilitate the matching of finance, technology, and capacity-building support to these actions; to take the collective commitment by developed countries to provide new and additional resources and to establish a Green Climate Fund.

In 2011, Durban Summit (COP17) was held in Durban, South Africa. The summit was successful to produce a binding international agreement by 2020 as follows: REDD-plus; climate cha nge finance; measurement, reporting and verification standards, CDM; technology transfer and development, capacity building, phasing out the fossil fuels subsidies, and introducing a levy on aviation and shipping; land use, land-use changes, and forestry; adaptation; mitigation; market solutions and scientific review process.

Lastly, a fifth assessment report (AR5) in 2014 had argued human influence on the climate system between 1951-2010 and the increasing likelihood of severe, pervasive, and irreversible impacts due to the increasing magnitude of warming. IPCC (2014) explained that adaptation to future climate change leads to reduce vulnerability and exposure to present climate variability and the overall risks of climate change impacts decreases while at the limit of the rate and magnitude of climate change.

Besides, in 1987, Montreal Protocol captured this issue related to ozone layer depletion through the limitation of using halogenated hydrocarbons. Furthermore, the United Nations through the Brund land Commission (the World Commission on Environment and Development) followed this issue in 1987. The commission endorsed the concept of sustainable development for the first time in the book, Our Common Future. The concept of sustainable development had expanded on the international level after the United Nations Conference on Environment and Development held in Rio de Janeiro in 1992. The world summit on sustainable development was held in Johannesburg in 2002. IPCC's Fourth Assessment Report in 2007 focused on human influence on our changing climate, like the world summit.

UNEP released the Global Glacier Changes-Facts and Figures in 2008 focusing on the fluctuations of glaciers and ice caps. The report confirms the double average annual melting rate of glaciers since the turn of the millennium. Further, UNEP Year Book 2009 had followed again ice loss from ice sheets and glaciers.

In 2014, IPCC (2014) released AR5 Synthesis Report: Climate Change 2014 including AR5 Climate Change 2013: The Physical Science Basis, AR5 Climate Change 2014: Impacts, Adaptation and Vulnerability, and AR5 Climate Change 2014: Mitigation of Climate Change. Since 2007, the working team was working on climate change issues. The report mentions that human influence on the climate system is clear and recent anthropogenic emissions of GHG are the highest in history. Recent climate changes have had widespread impacts on human and natural systems. In case of future risk, the report notes GHG accumulation changes in all components of the climate system, increasing the likelihood of severe, pervasive, and irreversible impacts for people and ecosystems. Adaptation and mitigation are complementary strategies for reducing and managing the risks of climate change. Substantial emissions reductions over the next few decades can reduce climate risks in the $21^{st}$ century and beyond, increase prospects for effective adaptation, reduce the costs and challenges of mitigation in the longer term, and contribute to climate-resilient pathways for sustainable development.

## CONCEPT OF CLIMATE CHANGE

Current studies have found climate variability at the global level. This is verified by the fact of changing heterogeneous climatic variables such as temperature, sea level, rain, glacier melting, coastal cyclone, etc. recorded by different climatic monitoring centers of the world. Studies Ramos-Martin (2001a), Watkiss et al. (2005), Owen and Hanley (2004), Ravindranath and Sathaye (2003), and reports of IPCC (2001) and UNFCCC (2002a) explained global climate change in a scientific assessment. IPCC (2001) argues that most of the warming (of 0.1 °C per decade) observed over the last 50 years is attributable to human activity. The Intergovernmental Panel on Climate Change (IPCC) stated that "warming of the climate system is unequivocal, as is now evident from observations of increases in global average air and ocean temperatures, widespread melting of snow and ice, and rising global mean sea level" (IPCC, 2007, p. 4).  Salinger (2005) supplemented with the trend of climate variability in the twenty-first century as follows: a) the regular rapid temperature increases in high latitudes of Northern Hemisphere, b) drying in Mediterranean areas, and c) increasing climate variability especially in sub-tropical and tropical latitudes.  Hansen and Ruedy (2011) found that the average annual temperature was larger in the winter hemisphere than in the summer and larger over land than over the ocean. Its reason was the huge difference in temperature low latitude and high latitudes in winter.

Similarly, Owen and Hanley (2004) explained it as a global public bad, in which both physical and economic actions and their feedback determines potential risks for human and the environment. In their paper, they say it as the classic example of a global stock externality–the flow of greenhouse gas (GHG) emissions accumulate into a global carbon stock that poses risks to humanity around the globe.  Ravindranath and Sathaye (2003) note it as one of the most important global environmental challenges challenging humanity with implications for food production, natural ecosystems, fresh water supply, health, etc. Climate change represents a considerable policy challenge (IPCC, 2007). UNFCCC (2007) establishes the adverse relationship between climate change and human activity by stating that climate change refers to a change of climate affecting directly or indirectly to human activity that changes the composition of the global atmosphere and then to natural climate variability observed over comparable periods. USGCS (2007) has pointed out similar but specifically noted that climate affects every dimension of life on earth including human health and well-being and also agriculture, water, and energy resources.

Stern (2006) argued its vertical and horizontal distribution all over the World. Its impact depends on the variation on adaptation capacity and behavior as well as mitigation activity among countries. In this literature Stern (2006) and IPCC (2001a), the developing countries are socio-economically more vulnerable than developed countries based on adaptive capacity and behavior. Furthermore, its adversities can be found in human activity: production, consumption, and development activity. Measuring such adversities in different sectors is studied by Hassan (2008), Hanif, Syed, Ahmad and Malik (2010), Joshi and Thapa (2010), Kurukulasuriya and Ajwad (2004), Mendelsohn, Nordhaus and Shaw (1994), Mirza and Schmitz (2011), Seo, Mendelsohn, Dinar, Hassan and Kurukulasuriya (2009), Seo and Mendelsohn (2008),

Shrestha, Maharjan and Joshi (2012). Most of the literature in agriculture (Kurukulasuriya and Ajwad (2004), K.C. (2013), and Seo and Mendelsohn (2008)) have focused on the impact of climate change empirically estimated by three popular approaches: a) Agricultural processing approach, b) Ricardian approaches and c) Profit functional approach.

Climate change directly affects agricultural production, as agriculture is integrally delicate to climate conditions and is one of the most vulnerable sectors to the risks and impact of global climate change (Parry, Canziani, Palutikof, Van der Linde and Hanson, 2007). Effects of climate change such as decreasing food production, leading to the higher price level, and vulnerability to the poor are different from region to region, Average crop yields in Pakistan are expected to 50 percent drop. In Nepal, it is an estimated 20 percent drop. According to IPCC (2001), the global community is facing the impact of climate change both now and in the future. Additionally, it is widely recognized that the severest impacts are more likely to be experienced in developing countries (largely due to the low capacity of populations to adapt coupled with fragile infrastructure). There is a higher expectation of a negative impact on Nepal.

**Chapter Three**

# CLIMATE CHANGE IN SOUTH ASIA

This chapter presents the conditions of climate change and vulnerability in South Asia based on IPCC, UNFCCC, and South Asian climate change fact sheets through observation and projection methods. This chapter portrays climate change scenarios at present and the future from the real scenario, projection, and policy responses.

## CLIMATE CHANGE IN ASIA: OBSERVATION AND PROJECTION

Emerging climate change and its extremes are observed in South Asia. Stern (2006), IPCC (2008) and ADB (2018) have also similar observed. IPCC (2008) has reported increasing numbers of warm days and decreasing numbers of cold days in Asia, where 4299 million population (60 % of the world population) in 2013 lives in 51 countries/regions. These countries are heterogeneous in climate resilience across per capita income – more than 51079 USD per capita income in developed and developing countries and less than 1000 USD per capita income in the least developed countries. Since the massive population of least developing countries has less than 1000 USD per capita income, massive populations are vulnerable and non-resilient (WB, 2013). Climate change and its extremes are emerging drivers having adverse effects a massive population.

**Figure 1: Climate change in Asia**

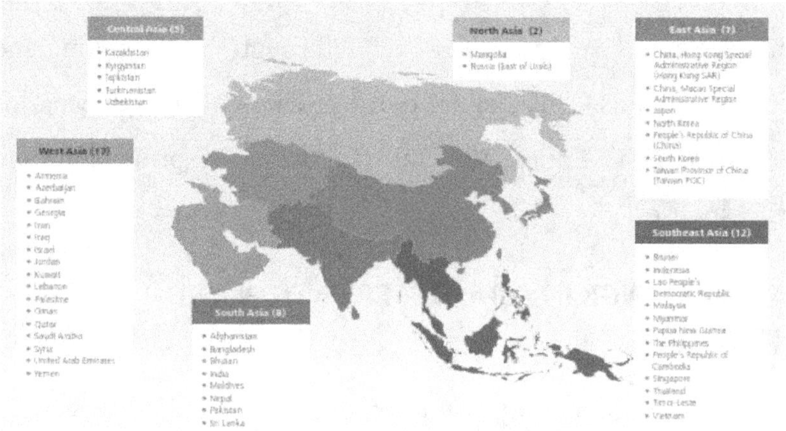

*Source: UNFCCC, 2014*

Based on different secondary information about climate change and its events in Asia(Figure 1), extreme climate change events are observed across Asia (IPCC, 2008) as follows:

- Precipitation factsheet (from 1900 to 2005) showed a significant increase in northern and central Asia but decreasing in parts of Southern Asia (Figure 1).
- Warming including higher extremes has increasing trends in Asia.

- Rapid melting of glaciers but water resources scarcity
- Risk of extinction for many plants and animal species in Asia as a result of the synergistic effects of climate change and habitat fragmentation
- Negative impact on food production
- Sea level rising damaged coastal ecosystems and foods of millions of populations
- Vulnerabilities of industry, infrastructure, settlements, and society to climate change at higher exposure areas, particularly coastal and riverine areas
- Temperature increasing across Southeast Asia at a rate of $0.14^0$c to $0.20^0$c per decade since the 1960s

The above extremes of climate change reveal the growth of climate change intensity in Asia where the massive vulnerable population lives (Figure 1).

## OBSERVED AND PROJECTED CLIMATE CHANGE IN ASIA

**Observed Climate Change** is based on measurable climatic parameters**:** *temperature, precipitation and monsoon, rainfall, glacier melting, and rising sea level.*

- **Temperature** is observed as **the** mean annual temperature to measure climate change. Metrological and hydrological monitoring shows its growing trend over the past century in most of Asia region, except high altitude areas. Its outcomes are increasing the number of warm days and nights and decreasing the number of cold days and nights across most of Asia since the 1950s, along with the growth of heat wave frequency since the middle of the 20th century in large parts of Asia (IPCC, 2008).

**Precipitation and Monsoons** are observed into trends and extremes. Metrological and hydrological monitoring indicates their strong variability with both increasing and decreasing trends of heavy precipitation events but in central Asia, no spatial coherent trends are found. In China, there was enhanced mean and extreme precipitation along the Yangtze River valley ($30^0N$) but deficient mean precipitation in North China in summer monsoon since the 1920s was also found in sea level pressure gradients (IPCC, 2008). Similarly, in West Asia, the mean precipitation trend was downward and weak, despite the growth of intense weather events. A similar trend was observed in South Asia with inter decadal variability with noticeably a declining trend with more frequent deficit monsoons under regional homogeneities. The increasing frequency of heavy precipitation events but light rain events are observed. In India, there was an increase in extreme rainfall events at the expense of weaker rainfall events over the central Indian region and in many other areas. In Peninsular Malaya, total rainfall and the frequency of wet days decreased but rainfall intensity increased in much of the region during the southwest monsoon season. During the northeast monsoon, total rainfall, the frequency of extreme rainfall events, and the rainfall intensity all increased over the peninsula (IPCC, 2008)

**Tropical and Extratropical Cyclones** are key climatic parameters to measure and indicate climate change and supplementation to all climatic indicators. These parameters are observed weak upward trends in the western North Pacific since the 1970s in the time series analysis of cyclones (WGI AR5 section 2.6.3). Surprisingly and interestingly, its reverse activity and intensity in northern Eurasia over the last 50 years (60°N to 40°N), including lower latitudes in East Asia (see WGI AR52.6.3).

**Monsoon is a good parameter of climate change. It is observed increase in mean precipitation in the East Asian summer monsoons in m**ore than 85% of CMIP5 models while more than 95% of models project an increase in heavy precipitation events (see WGI AR5 Section 14.2.2, Figure 14.4, IPCC, 2008). Almost all models indicate an increase in both the mean and extreme precipitation in the Indian summer monsoon in these two regions, the interannual standard deviation of seasonal mean precipitation also increases (IPCC, 2008).

**Surface Wind Speeds** indicate climate change. Its seasonal and annual mean winds are observed weak in the Tibetan region from around the 1960s or 1970s to the early 2000s (IPCC, 2008).

**Ocean level (Sea Level)** is a climatic parameter varying across different temperatures. Its significant growth of sea-level rise is observed in the central and eastern tropical Pacific over the period 1993 -2010 (IPCC, 2008). It is also observed in Asian regional sea levels.  In the Sea of Japan, its rise of 5.4± 0.3 mm yr is observed two times more than the global mean sea level from 1993 to 2001(Figure 2).  It is observed in the Indian sea (IPCC, 2008) mean significant wave heights are projected for the trade and monsoon wind regions of the Indian Ocean (IPCC, 2008).

## Figure 2: Observed Climate Change in Asia

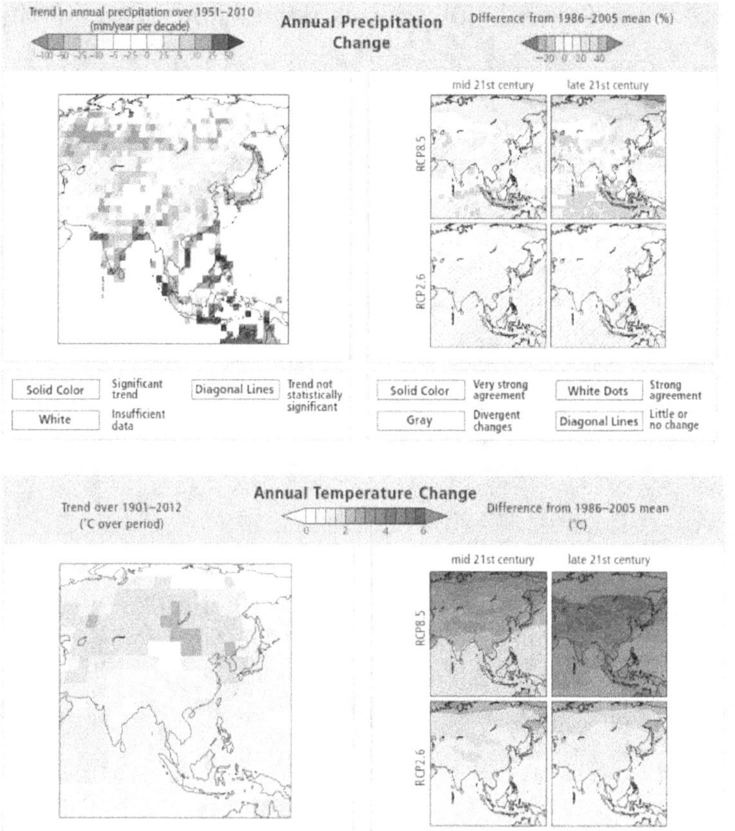

Figure 24-2 | Observed and projected changes in annual average temperature and precipitation in Asia. (Top panel, left) Map of observed annual average temperature change from 1901–2012, derived from a linear trend. (WGI AR5 Figures SPM.1 and 2.21) (Bottom panel, left) Map of observed annual precipitation change from 1951–2010, derived from a linear trend. (WGI AR5 Figures SPM.2 and 2.29) For observed temperature and precipitation, trends have been calculated where sufficient data permit a robust estimate (i.e., only for grid boxes with greater than 70% complete records and more than 20% data availability in the first and last 10% of the time period). Other areas are white. Solid colors indicate areas where trends are significant at the 10% level. Diagonal lines indicate areas where trends are not significant. (Top and bottom panel, right) CMIP5 multi-model mean projections of annual average temperature changes and average percent changes in annual mean precipitation for 2046–2065 and 2081–2100 under RCP2.6 and 8.5, relative to 1986–2005. Solid colors indicate areas with very strong agreement, where the multi-model mean change is greater than twice the baseline variability (natural internal variability in 20-yr means) and ≥90% of models agree on sign of change. Colors with white dots indicate areas with strong agreement, where ≥66% of models show change greater than the baseline variability and ≥66% of models agree on sign of change. Gray indicates areas with divergent changes, where ≥66% of models show change greater than the baseline variability, but <66% agree on sign of change. Colors with diagonal lines indicate areas with little or no change, where <66% of models show change greater than the baseline variability, although there may be significant change at shorter timescales such as seasons, months, or days. Analysis uses model data and methods building from WGI AR5 Figure SPM.8. See also Annex I of WGI AR5. (Boxes 21-2 and CC-RC)

## PROJECTED CLIMATE CHANGE

Climate change, an undesired disaster threat, is the most concern issue to the world because of its growth and its unpredictable uncertainties, and possible massive disasters and loss.  Stern (2006) raises what will happen in the next 50 years if in business as usual and if not in business as usual (mitigation measures). Despite the strong commitment of the International community to adopt mitigation measures, climate change is very likely as business as usual. The AR4 assessment predicted the consistent growth of warming in the 21st century (Christensen et al., 2007). In this prediction, Asia is not exceptional based on the Coupled Model Intercomparison Project Phase 5 (CMIP5) (IPCC, 2008).

In the 21st century, there is a prediction of mean annual temperature range from greater than 3°C over South and Southeast Asia to greater than 6°C over high latitudes in the late-21st century based on the 2°C above the late-20th-century baseline. Projections of future annual precipitation change are qualitatively similar to those assessed in the AR4 (Christensen et al., 2007).


**CLIMATE CHANGE IN SOUTH ASIA**

The South Asia region is called the Hindu Kush region spreading Himalayan peaks to the Indian peninsula to the Indian Ocean. In this region, Bhutan, Nepal, and Pakistan are located in the higher altitude, Bangladesh and India in the Indian peninsula and Sri Lanka and the Maldives in the Indian Ocean. This diverse landscape has divergent climatic variables, areas, zones, and regions across altitude and composition of natural phenomenon. Therefore, climate variation and its activity and effects are ice melting, glacier bursting, landslides, soil erosion, floods, forest fires, rising sea levels, tides, and saline water disturbance.

ADB (2018) in the assessment of the costs of climate change and adaptation in South Asia estimated about 9 percent economic loss of South Asian economy by the end of this century excluding the human and financial damage from floods, droughts, and other extreme weather events. Besides it, more than 600 million absolute poor-more than half of the world's total poor-living in the region depends on climate-sensitive sectors including agriculture, forestry, and traditional fishing for much of their day-to-day needs. With changes in the global climate system likely to span into the next century, geography, high population density, and immense poverty will continue to make South Asia especially vulnerable. Its stress on human health, biodiversity, agricultural production, food security, water, energy, and coastal settlements will be as migration on major cities. The report predicts that by 2050, the collective economy of six countries—Bangladesh, Bhutan, India, the Maldives, Nepal, and Sri Lanka - will lose an average of 1.8% of its annual gross domestic product, rising to 8.8% by 2100. These facts and projections depend on the collective action of the world community towards mitigation and adaptation. If the world community's action controls the rise in global temperatures below an average 2°C, then South Asia's economy would only be reduced by 1.3% annually by 2050 and 2.5% by 2100, and the cost of protecting itself from the worst of the impacts would be nearly halved. This region would be much more comfortable. It depends on the implementation of the Paris Climate Agreement in 2015.

In this South Asian region, there are identified climatic threats. According to recent studies by ICIMOD, there are 20 potentially dangerous glacial lakes in Nepal and 25 in Bhutan 3 posing the risk of outburst floods to outlying communities. India is also witnessing the formation and spread of glacial lakes. Similarly, coastal areas, overgrazed rangelands, and denuded mountains are particularly affected. In India, 26% of the coastline is prone to erosion, with 450 hectares of land lost every year. Sri

Lanka's coastline is subject to significant erosion in certain areas, while the hill country is prone to frequent landslides.

The region's long and heavily settled coastlines are seriously threatened by sea-level rise. In Bangladesh alone, the sea level is predicted to rise 45 centimeters by 2050, affecting 10%–15% of the land area and an estimated 35 million people. Sea level is also projected to rise by around 15–38 centimeters in India by 2050, placing major cities driving regional growth at risk, including Kochi, Kolkata, and Mumbai. A high proportion of Sri Lankan coastal land is less than 1 meter above sea level and could be submerged with the rising tides, along with critical transport infrastructure. The Maldives' very survival is in jeopardy, as the average height of its islands is 1.5 meters above sea level, and its highest point is less than 2 meters above sea level. The grave risks posed by sea-level rise could trigger large-scale migration, with ripple effects across borders. Sea-level rise gives way to saline water intrusion, threatening drinking water supply, agriculture, and aquaculture. In Bangladesh, more than 100 million hectares of arable land are affected. All of the Maldives are affected by saline water intrusion due to rising sea levels.

A flood is a threat to Bangladesh, India, Nepal, and Sri Lanka with heavy monsoon rains, blocked natural drainage, and melting glaciers. In 2007, abnormal monsoon rains caught South Asia unprepared to cope with the floods that affected an estimated 30 million people from Bangladesh, India, and Nepal. Thus, South Asia is extremely vulnerable to natural disasters, and a significant portion is exposed to more than one type of hazard. Between 1990 and 2008, more than 750 million people—50% of South Asia's population—were affected by at least one type of disaster, resulting in almost 230,000 deaths and about $45 billion in damages (WB, 2009).

As mentioned in UNFCCC, adaptation is a very important element. It includes three key milestones: the Least Developed Countries Work Program, the Nairobi Work Program, and the Cancun Adaptation Framework. Therefore, these South Asian countries of the Indian peninsula in the collaboration with ADB and WB have adopted adaptation action more than mitigation action for minimizing climate change impacts and loss as follows: improving institutional and human resource capacity to perceive, plan, and action related to adaptation and mitigation, integrity approach between climate-resilient policy and development ( climate-resilient transportation and urban development, clean energy promotion, climate-smart agriculture, industry and housing, conservation of forest and water and climate data management and analysis).

SAARC initiated to respond regionally to climate change threats. In 2007, SAARC perceived collectively it as a threat through the SAARC Declaration on Climate Change. In 2008, SAARC Dhaka Summits declared three years action plan against climate change. In 2010, SAARC Thimphu Summit set its targets of reducing carbon emission, promoting renewable energy, alleviating poverty, and strengthening climate-resilient communities. Member countries of SAARC have initiation to respond to climate change. Bangladesh established institutions related to climate change such as climate change cells (CCCs) in 2004 in relevant ministries and line agencies and climate change unit in 2010 in the Ministry of Environment and Forest. Simultaneously, NAPA was initiated in 2005 and updated in 2009. In 2008, Bangladesh implemented a climate change strategy and action plan with six priorities: food security, social protection and health, comprehensive disaster management, infrastructure development, research and knowledge management, mitigation and low-carbon development, and capacity building and strengthening institution under climate change fund. Similarly, Bhutan implemented National

Adaptation Program in 2006. Under vision 2020, Bhutan emphasized on mitigation approach through developing hydro and solar energy. Indeed, India focused on mitigation and adaptation under National Action Plan on climate change in 2008 as follows: solar energy, enhanced energy efficiency, sustainable habitat, water, sustaining the Himalayan ecosystem. For example, the Kerala Sustainable Urban Development project will improve infrastructure and services related to water and sanitation, drainage, solid waste management, and roads and transport. This will strengthen adaptive capacities and reduce greenhouse gas emissions as well.

In 2010, Nepal prepared NAPA and implemented LAPA. Before it, Nepal implemented three years interim sustainable development plan (2007-2010) focusing more on forest resource management and upgrading water infrastructure. In addition, climate change resilient policy is incorporated in all development Ministry and line agencies. Sri Lanka and the Maldives have also implemented NAPA and LAPA to respond to climate change. These policies of Sri Lanka develop renewable energy resources, energy efficiencies, carbon sequestration, waste management, infrastructure vulnerabilities, zoning, rainwater harvesting, and adaptation measures to increase vectors and food security measures. Meanwhile, Maldives identified 11 priority adaptation projects focused on coastal and coral reef protection, adaptation in agriculture, freshwater and fishery sectors, and food security and health.

# Chapter Four

# CLIMATE CHANGE IN NEPAL

This chapter focus on the assessment of climate change in Nepal based on empirical evidence of climate variation from 1980 to 2019. The climate variation is captured by analyzing the status and trend of climatic variables- temperature and rainfall based on real-time series data of temperature and rainfall, along with its projection. This chapter identifies how it will be extreme and how it will be a threat and risk in Nepal.

## CLIMATE CHANGE IN NEPAL

Climate change that is the variation state of climatic variables is a well-established Tran's boundary collective issue in the world perceived and endorsed by IPCC (2001) and UNFCC (2001) since 2001. Metrological and hydrological historical data of the world provides evidence of climate change in developing countries, like Stern (2006), Elisch (2008), and UNFCCC (2008). This South Asian country, Nepal is not exceptional from climate change.

Recent scientific studies have provided supplementary scientific evidence of climate change in Nepal. Disaster factsheets (MOHA, 2019) reveal the growth of disaster events (flood, fire, landslides, soil erosion, drought glacier bursting and flood, extinction of plants and species, etc). Similarly, the analysis of historical climatic data including temperature, rainfall, and disaster events over 50 years with the reference of climate change assessment approach developed by IPCC (2001) and UNFCCC (2001) was to respond its due gap about its issue, pattern, extremity, and adversity for exploring its potential responses. As a result, the historical trend of mean temperature shows the occurrence of unexpected variation per annum. A similar result is found in rainfall and precipitation. As annual supplementary evidence of extreme floods and landslides and their physical and economic losses and deaths, the state of the climate is observed variation in Nepal. Therefore, climate change is emerging as a well-established issue in Nepal.

Despite various climatic variables, two climatic parameters including temperature and rainfall are used to measure climate change. Both parameters are qualitatively and quantitatively measurable. Temperature is a quantitative measure of hot and cold (Oliver and Hidone, 1984 and Basnet, 1989). Its variation that can be found in the variation of altitude, location, and topography indicates warming of the country (Basnet, 1989 and Hare, 1953). Similarly, rainfall is another climatic parameter. Its variation also indicates climate change.

Climate variation occurs unevenly across a variety of altitudes and topography all over Nepal. The assessment of annual rainfall data over 50 years all over Nepal reveals the rainfall ranges from 50mm to 5000 mm in the different weathers across different altitudes and topography of Nepal (DHM, 2019). Mean annual rainfall that is estimated at 1857.6 mm measures the growth and distribution of warming levels. Above 5000 mm higher rainfall range is recorded in the southern slope of Makalu range in Eastern Development region, Jugal range in Central Development region and south of Annapurna range in Western Development region as low landscapes, meanwhile lower rainfall areas of below 143 mm are higher landscapes: Manang and Mustang (DHM, 2019). Thus, the relationship between rainfall and altitude is inverse that is the higher altitude, least rainfall, and the lower altitude, the higher rainfall. Similarly, such a relationship is observed between temperature and altitude. Its examples are the Mountain belt and Terai belt. The Mountain belt that is the highest altitude landscape with above 5000 meters has a lower temperature in both seasons: winter and summer meanwhile Terai belt that is the lowest altitude landscape in the range from 60 meters to 200 meters has a higher temperature in both seasons: winter and summer.

Table 2 provides evidence of that mountain (higher altitude) at less than $3^0$ C followed by hill (moderate altitude) at $10^0$ C -$15^0$ C and Terai (lower altitude) at $20^0$ C - $25^0$C. Thus, these findings of climatic variation across altitude from Terai to Mountain are similar with the findings of Basnet (1989).

**Table 2: Weather Distribution and Climatic variables**

| Season | Month | Precipitation | Rainfall | Temperature |
|---|---|---|---|---|
| Pre-monsoon | March-May | strong westerly wind prevails throughout Nepal | Scattered | $3^0$ C-$15^0$C |
| Monsoon | June-August | strong precipitation from the Bay of Bengal for these months | • 60-90%<br>• >400 cm in Central Nepal<br>• >200 cm in Eastern Nepal<br>• >250 cm in Western Nepal | $15^0$C-$25^0$C |
| Post Monsoon | September - November | Frequent fogs appear in the atmosphere | Scattered | $5^0$C-$15^0$C |
| Winter | December-February | Weak precipitation winds from the west to north Fog in the valley location (Kathmandu, Surkhet, Dang, etc.) | Scattered | $15^0$ C (below 3000 Meter) Freezing points (above 3000 Meter) |

Source: *Field Survey, 2015and DHM, 2019*

Climatically, climate variation and its characteristics and status are twisted with weather season: its patterns and cycles including summer, monsoon (pre-monsoon season (March-May), Monsoon season (June-September) and Post Monsoon Season (October-November)) and winter (DHM, 2019). The reverse relationship between temperature and rainfall can be observed in these seasons. In the summer season, temperature rises but rainfall decreases but in monsoon and post-monsoon seasons (winter), rainfall increases but temperature decreases. Thus, temperature and rainfall character and status vary across climatic seasons pattern and cycles. In recent scientific studies, the temperature in summer is observed extremely higher but rainfall is the least. In monsoon, the temperature is observed mild under extreme rainfall. In winter, the temperature is lower under lower rainfall, and snow falling is experienced (Table 2 & 3).

**Table 3: Ecological Distribution and Status**

| Ecological Belts | Climate | Rainfall (mm) | | Temp ($^0$C) |
|---|---|---|---|---|
| Mountain | Arctic /Alpine Artic/Alpine | Snow falling | 150 -200 | < 3-10 |
| Hill | Mixed (cool/warm) | 275-2300 | | 10-20 |
| Terai | Tropical/Sub Tropical | 1100-3000 | | 20-25 |

Source: *CST, 1997*

Rainfall depends on monsoon patterns and cycles (pre-monsoon, monsoon, post-monsoon, and winter). This cycle is naturally operated in a particular route. The growing warming level of the atmosphere adversely disturbs monsoon

**Figure 3: Precipitation Distribution**



Source: *DHM, 2019*

patterns and cycles. Therefore, its time, coverage, and intensity are experienced unlikely disturbance and undesired attributes. However, the intensity of rainfall is found extremely more in the monsoon season than pre-and post-monsoon and winter. Figure 3 illustrates the intensity of rainfall in which annual rainfall's shares of monsoon was 79.58 percent followed by 12.68 percent in pre-monsoon, 4.25 in post-monsoon, and 3.1 percent in winter. Nepal has had such rainfall patterns for a long time. In recent years, such intensity is consistent but its coverage, pattern, and length are observed in variation as part of climate change. Its adverse effects can be seen in the river system all over the country and household's socio-economic activities related to agriculture, industry, cleanliness and health, clean water supply, and drainage system.

## TREND AND PATTERN OF TEMPERATURE AND RAINFALL

**Descriptive Statistics of Temperature and Rainfall:** The time series data set of mean annual temperature $(^0c)$ and mean annual rainfall(mm) (1980-2019) was collected from the nine stations of Metrology and Hydrology for climate change analysis and measurement. The descriptive statistics tool is employed to analyze these two climatic variables: mean annual temperature and mean annual rainfall to sketch up the climate scenario of Nepal.

**Table 4: Descriptive Statistics of Temperature and Rainfall from 1980 to 2019**

| Indicator | Mean temp(0c) | Mean rainfall(mm) |
|---|---|---|
| Mean | 18.99 | 158.5 |
| Std. Deviation | 2.29 | 19.7 |
| Variance | 5.27 | 391.23 |
| Minimum | 12 | 120.7 |
| Maximum | 21 | 214.4 |

Source: *DHM, 2019*

Table 4 shows $19^0C$ mean annual temperature from 1980 to 2019 in Nepal where the minimum temperature is $12^0C$ and maximum temperature is $21^0C$. Its variance is $5.27^0C$ over the 40 years long period. This variance is evidence of inclining mean annual temperature by $1.31^0C$ per decade (Table 4). Thus, Nepal has witnessed slow and gradual climate variation towards extremity until this threat will be minimized.

**Table 5: Descriptive Statistics of Annual Temperature across Stations**

| Stations | N | Range | Min | Max | Mean | Std. Deviation | Variance |
|---|---|---|---|---|---|---|---|
| Taplejung | 40 | 41 | -23 | 18 | 15.10 | 7.03 | 49.44 |
| Biratnager | 40 | 10 | 15 | 25 | 24.30 | 1.75 | 3.06 |
| Hetauda | 40 | 22 | 22 | 43 | 23.68 | 3.58 | 12.81 |
| Pokhara | 40 | 2 | 20 | 22 | 21.09 | .51 | .266 |
| Bhirahawa | 40 | 10 | 15 | 25 | 24.52 | 1.69 | 2.86 |
| Jomsom | 40 | 56 | -44 | 12 | 8.40 | 10.41 | 108.50 |
| Surkhet | 40 | 6 | 17 | 23 | 21.64 | .92 | .852 |
| Jumla | 40 | 3 | 11 | 14 | 12.81 | .59 | .352 |
| Dhangadi | 40 | 54 | -30 | 24 | 18.11 | 12.10 | 146.53 |

Source: *DHM, 2019*

Table 5 shows 160.35 mm mean annual rainfall from 1980 to 2019. Over the 40 years long period, its variance is 383.26 mm. Thus, it indicates decreasing rainfall per annum. It also supplements to the variance of mean annual temperature indicating climate variance of Nepal.

In climate change, the variance distribution of mean annual temperature all over Nepal is uneven due to the growth of human-induced emission activities and the existence of natural exogenous and endogenous variables. From the Terai belt (lower altitude) to the Mountain belt (higher altitude), its distribution is found

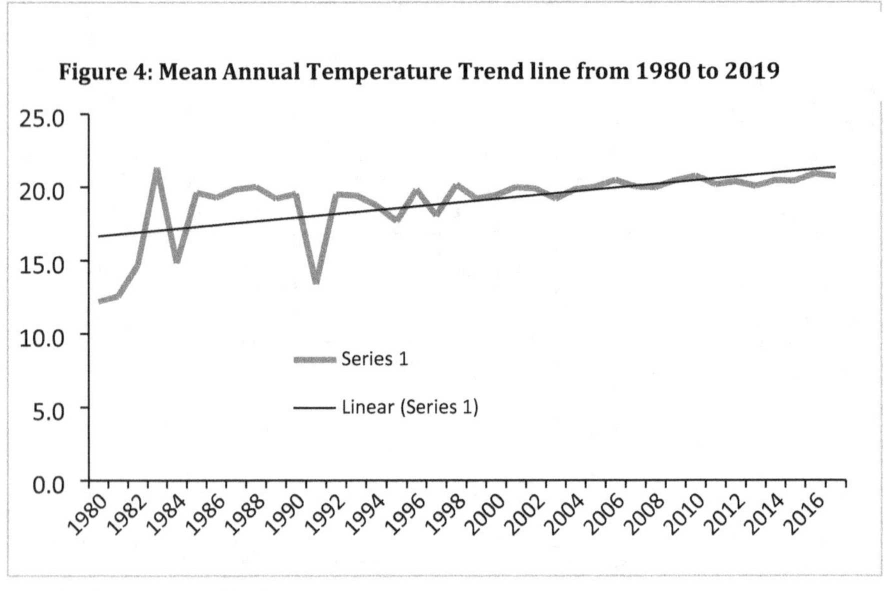



Source: *DHM, 2019*

unevenly. Lower variance of mean annual temperature is estimated in Pokhara (0.26$^0$C), Jumla(0.35$^0$C), Surkhet(0.85$^0$C), Bhairawaha(2.86$^0$C) and Biratnagar (3.06$^0$C) meanwhile its higher variance is estimated in Heatuda(12.81$^0$C), Taplejung(49.44$^0$C), Jomsom (108.5$^0$C), and Dhangadhi(146.53$^0$C). However, Dhanghadi, a low landscape has the highest variance at 146.53, and Pokhara, a moderate landscape has the lowest variance at

0.266. Thus, Dhanghadi has higher climate change than Pokhara. Vertically and horizontally, climate variation across all altitudes of nine metrological and hydrological stations spreads all over the country.

As supplementary, trend analysis of mean annual temperature from 1980 to 2019 is employed to observe its pattern and variance (Figure 4). Till 2010, its trend line is increasing above the trend line. After 2010, its variance and pattern are positively increasing below the trend line. The estimation of coefficient "β" provides a 0.12 value over a year. In Figure 4, the Linear Trend line of mean annual temperature shows $R^2 = 0.37$ as good fitness of line, coefficient (a) = 16. $53^0$C and coefficient of time (b) = $0.12^0$ C. The sign of the coefficient of time shows a positively inclining trend with $0.12^0$ C per additional year over 40 years. Visibly and invisibly, the marginal change of mean annual temperature is 0.12 in Nepal. Its growth depends on the achievement of NAPA and LAPA of Nepal. If their achievements areas targeted, marginal change of mean annual temperature will be either controlled or minimized. How much we can control, so much the society will be climate change resilient.

## Trend and Pattern of Temperature and Rainfall

**Figure 5: Mean National Monthly Temperature of 1980 and 2017**

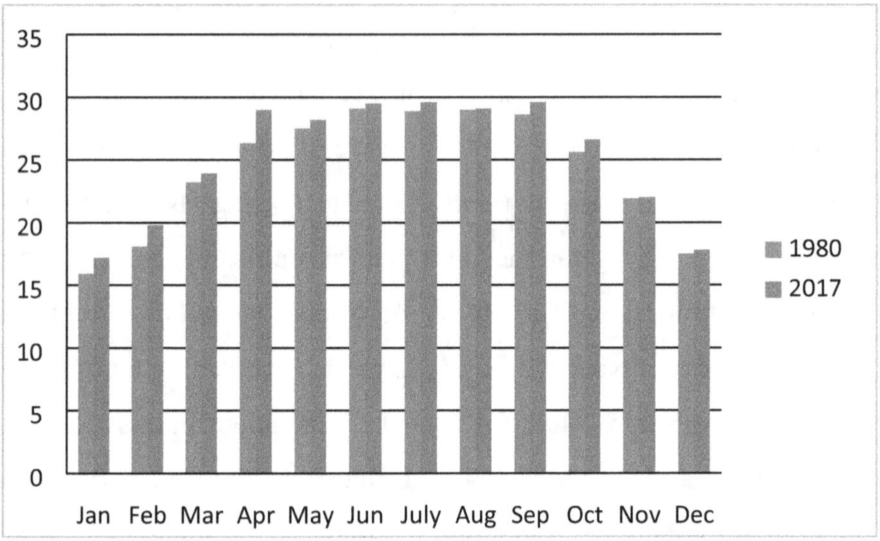

*Source: DHM, 2019*

Mean monthly temperature data of two periods: the period I (1980) and period II (2019) collected from nine metrological and hydrological stations is collected and compiled to understand the movement and momentum of mean monthly temperature over 40 years gap (Figure 5).  Except for August month, all months from January to December have positively inclining mean temperature between the period I (1980) and the period II (2019) (Figure 5). It illustrates increasing warm days not only in summer but also in the winter season. Over 40 years, mean monthly temperature growth is higher in January, February, April, September, and October. It means a higher warming level in these months. However, the mean monthly temperature is moderate in March, May, June, July, November, and December. In winter, the warming level is modest to reduce cold days (Figure 5). Thus, the reflection of climate change can be found noticeable in all months over 12 months, except August month. Therefore, Nepal has increasing warming days and decreasing cold days.

**Temperature by Station**

The sample stations of metrology and hydrology have delivered

**Figure 6: Stationwise Mean National Temperature from 1980 to 2019**

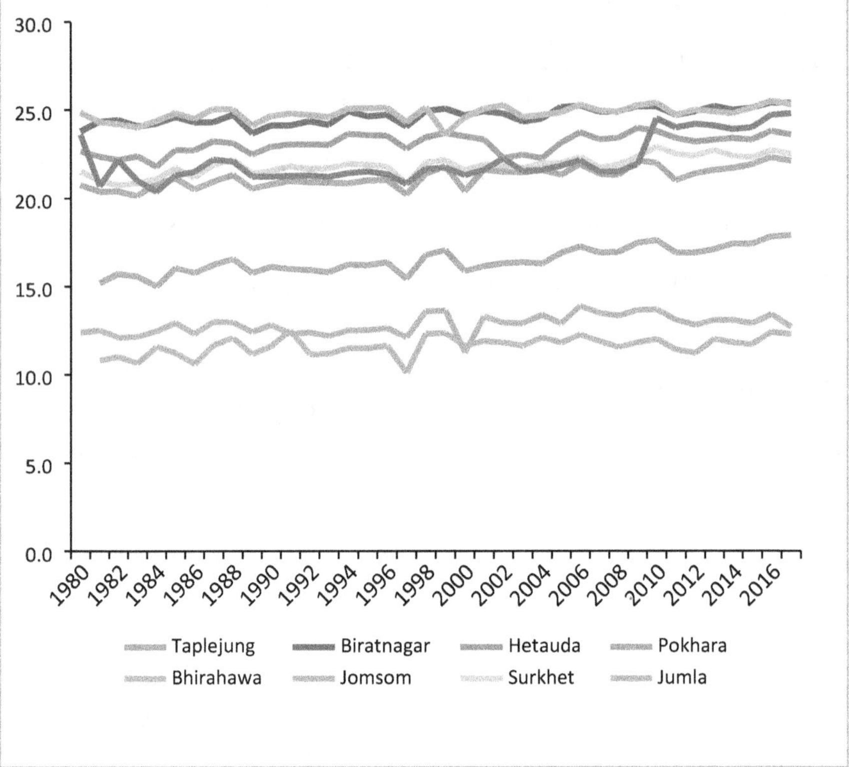


*Source: DHM, 2019*

time series data of annual temperature from 1980 to 2019. The trend line of every metrology and hydrology station indicates a gradual and slight positive momentum of annual temperature at different ranges (Figure 6). Therefore, climate variation occurs across the country, Nepal.

Similarly, rainfall is another climatic parameter of climate change. When temperature either increases or decreases, rainfall will either decrease or increase. Thus, rainfall has inversely related to temperature. Therefore, the temperature rising in Nepal illustrates itself decreasing rainfall.

The time-series data set of mean annual rainfall (mm) (1980-2019) was collected from the nine stations of Metrology and Hydrology for climate change analysis and measurement through rainfall pattern, trend, and intensity. The trend analysis tool is employed to analyze trends and patterns of mean annual rainfall to capture the climate scenario of Nepal (Figure 7). This analytical and explorative knowledge is relevant to about 67 percent dependency on agriculture in which the productivity and production of about 60 percent cultivated land and more than 40 percent of small landholder's livelihood security and welfare depends on rainfall's pattern, trend, and intensity, although irrigation development receives annually top priority with a huge budget allocation. In addition, about 80 percent rural population of Nepal uses wildly and widely fresh water collected in lakes and rivers for drinking, cleaning, and bathing, although the municipality building policy of Nepal has made prerogative and propaganda all rural villages in the municipality city without a systematic plan.

Figure 7 shows a fluctuating momentum pattern of annual rainfall from 1995 to 2019. Its trend line illustrates the declining trend of rainfall will -16.39 mm marginal change per annum across all seasons from monsoon to summer and winter. Rainfall was 2000 mm in 1995. Its status was 1674.5 mm in 2017. Over 22 years gap, rainfall has decreased by -325.5 mm, despite maximum rainfall of 1998, 2003, 2007, 2010, and 2013. Thus, it indicates climate variation in Nepal, along with emerging the growth of drought and water crisis for clean drinking and irrigation and higher possibility of livelihood crisis of the massive poor.

We have a curiosity about its marginal change per annum to understand the decreasing rate of rainfall per annum. The linear regression model is applied to explore and analyze rainfall patterns and trends. In Figure 7, the linear trend line of mean annual rainfall shows $R^2 = 0.30$ as a good fitness of line, coefficient (a) =2025.9 mm, and coefficient of time (b) = -16.39 mm. The sign of the

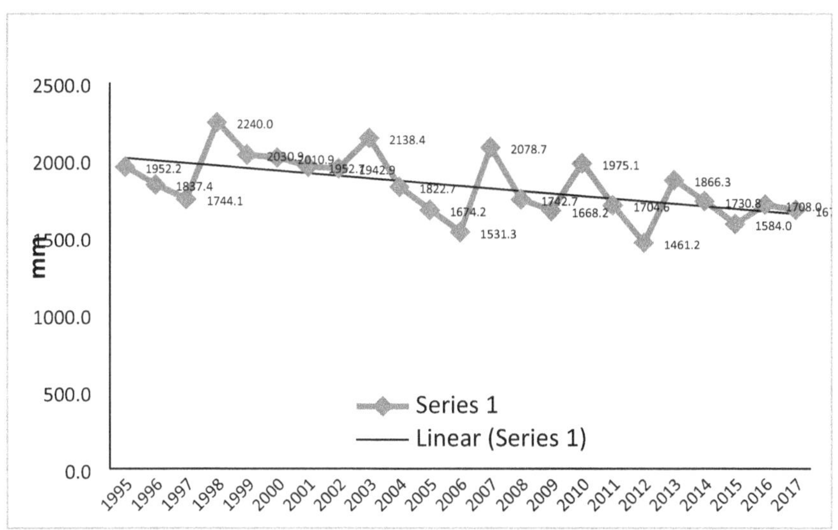


coefficient of time shows a negative trend with 16.39 mm per additional year over 23 years. Thus, decreasing rainfall is evidence of the climate change of Nepal. Thus, warming days are increasing overall year towards extremity until this threat will be minimized.

The difference to Difference method is used to analyze the time series annual rainfall data set (1995-2017) between three points:

**Figure 7: Mean National Rainfall from 1980 to 2019**

period I (1995), period II (2012), and period III (2017) to understand what is a difference of rainfall between these periods. The time series annual rainfall data set (1995-2017) was collected from nine sample metrology and hydrology stations.

The difference to difference method finds negative difference (decreasing) rainfall recorded in all stations. Except Hetuda, Bhairahwa and Tapeljung, all stations -Jomsom, Jumla, Pokhara, Dhangadhi, Morang and Surkhet have negative rainfall. The figure shows a negative difference in rainfall in Jomsom (-156.6mm), Jumla (-131 mm), Pokhara (1111.7mm), Dhangadhi (-524.6), Morang (-628.8 mm), and Surkhet (-157mm), except Hetuda (155.6 mm), Bhairahwa (17.72mm) and Taplejung (39.6 mm) (Figure 8). Changing the mean annual rainfall pattern and trend of Nepal that is evidence of climate change across Nepal will be a big threat of water crisis as disappearing lakes and small streams and decreasing water sources and water level of big rivers in future. As a result, livelihood sources of rural and urban populations will be unexpectedly so critical that poverty and vulnerability will be multiple.

**Figure 8: Mean National Rainfall from 1995 to 2019**



*Source: DHM, 2019*

**Table 6: Economic & Human Loss from 2000 to 2018**

| Year | Flood & Landslide | Thunder-bolt | Fire | Hail-stone | Wind-storm | Avalanche/Snow-storm | Epidemics | Earthquake | Total |
|---|---|---|---|---|---|---|---|---|---|
| 2000 | 173 | 26 | 37 | 1 | 2 | . | 141 | 0 | 380 |
| 2001 | 196 | 38 | 26 | 1 | 1 | . | 154 | 1 | 417 |
| 2002 | 441 | 6 | 11 | 0 | 3 | . | 0 | 0 | 461 |
| 2003 | 232 | 62 | 16 | 0 | 20 | . | 0 | 0 | 330 |
| 2004 | 131 | 10 | 10 | 0 | 0 | . | 0 | 0 | 151 |
| 2005 | 141 | 18 | 28 | 0 | 0 | 21 | 41 | 0 | 249 |
| 2006 | 141 | 15 | 3 | 1 | 0 | | 34 | 0 | 194 |
| 2007 | 216 | 40 | 9 | 13 | 1 | 6 | 0 | 0 | 290 |
| 2008 | 134 | 16 | 11 | 0 | 2 | 0 | 3 | 0 | 166 |
| 2009 | 135 | 7 | 35 | 0 | 0 | 2 | 10 | 0 | 189 |
| 2010 | 240 | 70 | 69 | 0 | 2 | 2 | 462 | 0 | 845 |
| 2011 | 263 | 95 | 46 | 2 | 6 | 0 | 36 | 0 | 448 |
| 2012 | 123 | 119 | 77 | 0 | 18 | 9 | 9 | 6 | 361 |
| 2013 | 219 | 146 | 39 | 0 | 3 | 7 | 4 | 0 | 438 |
| 2014 | 211 | 96 | 62 | 0 | 3 | 18 | 12 | 0 | 452 |
| 2015 | 293 | 115 | 53 | 0 | 2 | 2 | 18 | 9366 | 9848 |
| 2016 | 297 | 105 | 85 | 0 | 4 | 0 | 14 | 0 | 505 |
| 2017 | 236 | 85 | 63 | 0 | 5 | 1 | 10 | 0 | 400 |
| 2018 | 105 | 68 | 89 | 0 | 45 | 19 | 0 | 0 | 326 |
| Total | 3957 | 1137 | 789 | 23 | 117 | 107 | 948 | 9373 | 16451 |

*Source: Ministry of Home, Nepal, 2019*

Disaster events and losses in Nepal that are floods and landslides, thunder, fire, windstorm, etc are another parameter group of climate change and its economic loss. Over a year, disasters have cycled from Mountain to Terai belts (Table 6). Let's observe such a cycle, we can find snow melting and glacier bursting at Mountain and fire at Terai in the summer season, flooding and landslides at Hill and Terai region in monsoon season and snow falling in Mountain, freezing at Hill and cold wind at Terai in winter. It is reported that disaster events that have gradual growth per annum have become more disastrous in terms of human loss and economic loss over the last 40 years period. This consequence is due to the positive correlation between climate change and disasters. How much climate change happens in the future, so many disasters will be magnificent and multiple.

## CLIMATE CHANGE IN SURKHET

This section explores climate change and its climatic variable's pattern, trend, intensity, and impact in western Nepal specifically Surkhet as the district of the Sotkhola water basin and its catchment areas. Above mentioned parameters: temperature and rainfall are observed exploratively and analytically to capture momentum, characteristics, and status of climate change scenario.

## MEAN ANNUAL RAINFALL: TREND AND PATTERN

Concerning national climate change, Surkhet may not be the exceptional district in the context of emerging climate change, although this district enriches with natural catalysts and filters and with poor human-induced emissions related to primitive economic activities. About 40 percent small farmers population are struggling painfully for livelihood survival and against painful vulnerability and poverty level. Therefore, this climate change threat may be magnificent of poverty and vulnerability in this district. Therefore, Surkhet is sensitive to the threat of climate change. In this context, this assessment may be relevant to understand its nature, pattern, intensity, characteristics, sensitiveness, and impacts so that climatic induced poverty and vulnerability could be responded well with appropriate cost-effective innovative ideas, knowledge, and technology.

Like a national reference of climate change, climatic parameters: rainfall and temperature (1995-2019) were collected from the metrology and hydrology station of Birendranagar, Surkhet with the assumption of their variance. Before 1995, there was no rainfall time-series data set. In addition, the perception of the local population in the study area accepted undesirably to climate-induced disaster events and its big losses. Trend and status analysis tools were employed to measure rainfall variance over the past 23 years.

**Figure 9: Mean Rainfall Trend of Surkhet from 1995 to 2019**

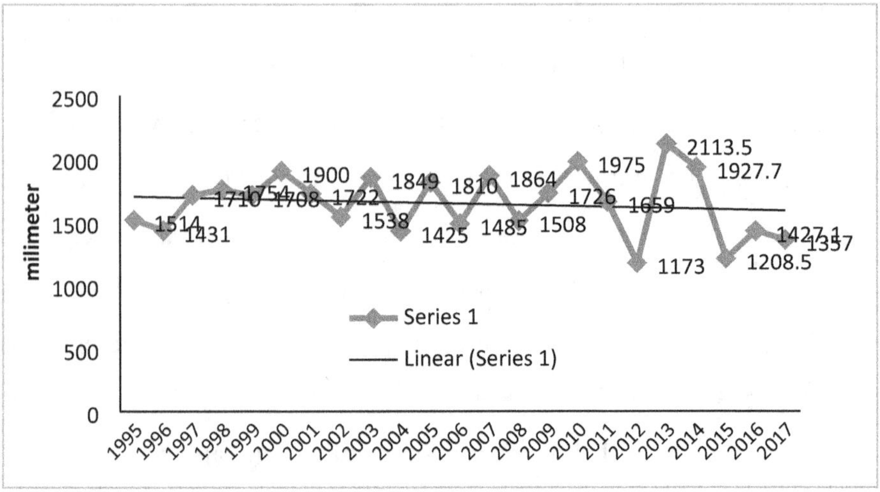

*Source: DHM, 2019*

Figure 9 shows the mean annual rainfall trend line (1995-2019) over the past 23 years long period in Surkhet. Like a national mean annual rainfall trend line, the trend line of the mean annual rainfall of Surkhet is decreasing from 1995 to 2017 with -5.06 mm. However, the movement line of mean annual rainfall fluctuates. It started with 1431 mm rainfall in 1996. The rainfall in 1999, 2003, 2005, 2007, 2011, and 2013 was above the trend line of mean annual rainfall but the rainfall in 1995, 1996, 1997, 1998, 2000, 2001, 2002, 2004, 2006, 2008, 2009, 2010, 2012, 2014, 2015, 2016 and 2017 was below the trend line. Difference to difference method to two periods: period I (1995) and period II (2017) shows decreasing rainfall with -157 mm. In addition, the difference between maximum mean annual rainfall (2113.5 mm) in 2013 and minimum mean rainfall (1173 mm) in 2012 was also negative with 940.5 mm.    Despite the fluctuation, the trend of mean annual rainfall in Surkhet has been declining, like its national trend line.

Figure 9 shows the linear trend line of the mean annual rainfall of Surkhet having $R^2 = 0.019$ as poor good fitness of line, coefficient (a) = 1703.6 mm, and coefficient of time (b) = -5.06 mm.    The sign of marginal change coefficient of time shows a negative trend with -5.06 mm per additional year over 23 years. The declining trend of mean annual rainfall indicates climate change in Surkhet.

The monthly mean rainfall parameter shows rainfall pattern and intensity overall year. Generally, rainfall intensity is higher in the monsoon season than in the summer and in the winter season. This parameter explores the change of rainfall pattern and intensity in Surkhet. The difference to difference method is employed by including three time periods: period I (1957), period II (1977), and period III (2014) to find out what is a change between period II (1977) and period III (2014) and what is its direction.

Despite declining rainfall over the past 37 years, changing mean monthly rainfall patterns and intensity are observed. In 2014, monthly rainfall was increasing in the following months: January, February, March, June, July, August, and December more than monthly rainfall in 1977, except the following months: May, April, September, and October. In 1977, the monsoon started from June to October. Its intensity was only in four months: July, August, September, and October. However, in 2014, its intensity was only three months: July, August, and September. There were record break rainfalls in July with 646.8 mm and August with 799.0 mm. However, in 1977, rainfall intensities in July and August were 188 mm and 196 mm. In September, its intensity was 313.7 mm but was 162.4 mm in 2014. Despite the fluctuation in rainfall intensity, rainfall intensity was found to increase over 17 years (Figure 10). Monthly rainfall details were presented in Figure 10.

Source: *DHM, 2017*

# TREND AND PATTERN OF MEAN ANNUAL TEMPERATURE IN SURKHET

Like as mean annual rainfall parameter, the mean annual temperature that is a key parameter to measure the growth of warming over a year is considered as a complementary cum supplementary parameter to rainfall to crosscheck its validity, reliability, and accuracy. This is widely practiced by scholars in climate science for reaching scientific output and outcome, like as by the social scientist. Therefore, this study has employed the mean annual temperature parameter to explore climate change and its nature, characteristics, pattern, intensity, and impacts in Surkhet.

Like as mean annual rainfall data set, the mean annual temperature time series data set (1980-2017) was collected from the hydrology and metrology station of Birendrangar, Surkhet to analyze its trend and pattern to understand climate change in Surkhet.

Figure 11 shows the fluctuated mean annual temperature observed line over the last 37 years long period in Surkhet. This observed mean annual temperature was fluctuating but inclining. In 1980, its range was at $21^0$C. After 37 years, it reached $22.2^0$C. Thus, the growth of temperature has made Surkhet warmer than before. It does not indicate climate stability. In addition, its minimum extreme point was 17 $^0$C in 2003 and its maximum extreme point was at $22.9^0$C in 2010. Thus, its fluctuation range was approximately $5.9^0$C over the last 37 years period. It provides strong evidence of increasing temperature or warming in Surkhet.

Despite the fluctuation, the trend of mean annual temperature in Surkhet is inclining, like as a national trend. In Figure 11, linear trend line of mean annual rainfall of Surkhet shows $R^2 = 0.62$ as poor good fitness of line, coefficient (a) = $21.12^0C$ and coefficient of time (b) = $0.038^0C$. The sign of the coefficient of time shows a trend with $0.038^0C$ per additional year over the last 37 years period. Thus, its trend line supplements its per annum temperature rising with $0.038^0C$. Surkhet is also sensitive to climate change threats. In this case, rural and mountain villages, so-called municipality cities may have water stress and disasters event due to disappearing water sources and decreasing water level of lakes and streams, along with glacier melting and bursting induced floods and landslides. Vulnerable rural populations, children, old age, and women may be more vulnerable to climate change, along with disturbance of agricultural productivity and production, the growth of livelihood struggle, and migration for livelihood. Thus, poverty and vulnerability of massive population in Surkhet may expand till such variation will be stabilized through minimizing human-induced emission-related economic activities and livelihood activities.

**Figure 11: Mean Temperature of Surkhet from 1980 to 2017**

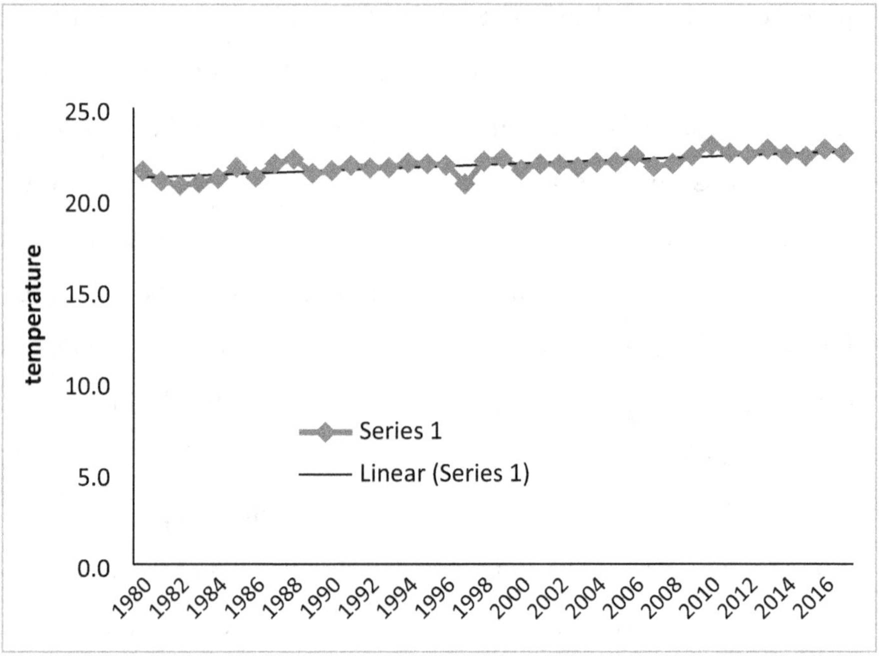


Source: *DHM, 2019*

Since monthly mean temperature measures to mean temperature's intensity and pattern, this analysis was used to measure month basis status and pattern of the mean temperature of Surkhet. Figure 12 shows $28^0$c maximum mean temperature recorded from May to September and $10^0$c minimum temperature recorded from December to February. Thus, the hottest months have been increasing, although temperature rising was below mean temperature rising in January, February, March, May, April, June, and July. Drought has been recorded to start quickly and to stay long in the watershed areas. In the winter season, there were only two months December and January in which there was increasing temperature more than mean temperature. During these months, the minimum temperature has been increasing. It means decreasing cold days with increasing warming days.

**Figure 12: Monthly Temperature & Mean Temperature (1980-2017)**

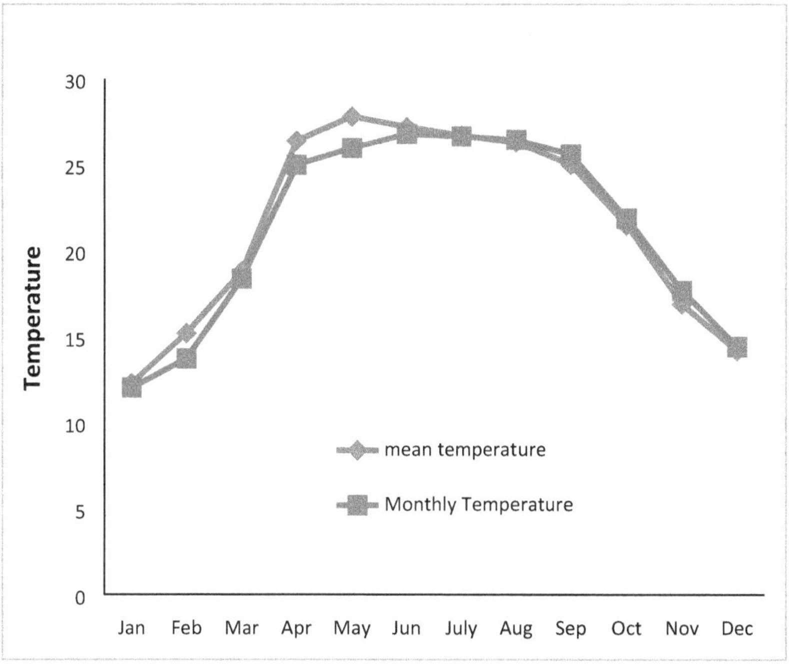

Source: *DHM, 2019*

Experience is a good teacher and the best source of knowledge. At the grassroots level, local households and communities across Surkhet have interesting and surprising experiences with various movements of climatic variables: temperature, rainfall, and disasters and their momentum in different seasonal cycles of heterogenous time (Table 7). Most communities of Gadhi, Lekhagaon, and Kunathari have bad experiences of heat stress in summer, cold stress in winter, flood and landslides disasters for their comfort and security over a year (Table 7).  Like other Nepalese people, they have as part and parcel of their life and livelihood.  These experiences were key sources of information and knowledge to verify the results of the above empirical analysis of descriptive statistics and trend analysis of mean annual temperature and rainfall.  The study was to collect such information from the local community through focused group discussion (FGD) and key informant information (KII) in Surkhet, specifically Gadhi, Kunathari, and Lekhagaon in 2015 to understand the climatic variable difference between two time periods (2000 and 2015) for responding whether Surkhet would have climate change and the level of poverty and vulnerability. All these valuable experiences and information of two periods: period I (2000) and period II (2015) are presented in the tabulate form in Table 7.

**Table 7: Climate change in local areas**

| Indicators | Past time Period (2000) | Present time period (2015) |
|---|---|---|
| Temperature | | |
| Event | none | extreme |
| Nature | not so | increasing |
| Type | | |
| Time period | day time | day time (morning time) |
| Rainfall | | |
| Event | no extreme | extreme |
| Nature | no intense | intense |
| Type | all areas | patch areas |
| Time period | 7 days long | 3 days long |
| | April 28-May 29 (Basikha 15-Jestha 15) | May 29-June 22(Jestha 15-Asad 7) |
| Snow falling | Yes (three days in Gadhi in 1990) | No |
| Hailstorm | more | less |
| Drought | less due to active water sources | higher due to dryness of water sources |

Source: *Field Survey, 2015 and Key Informant, 2015*

Scientifically, rainfall is the source of water in the earth whatever its form as sea, river, lake, pond, etc., along with the indigenous knowledge and experience of the local community. As a result, rainfall and water availability have a positive correlation. When rainfall's pattern, intensity, and duration vary naturally and unnaturally, the water level of sea, lake, and river will vary expectedly and unexpectedly. Its outcomes will be negative to human-induced activities (agriculture, industrial, and service), biodiversity of the earth, and human needs (clean drinking water for households and livestock). Thus, climate change experience was found interestingly.

Table 7 shows changing temperature, rainfall, hailstorm, snow falling, and drought between period I (2000) and period II (2015) as the memory of the local community of three sample catchments areas: Gadhi, Kunathari, and Lekhagaon. Almost all community who live on the top of hills told their common experience of changing temperature momentum and patterns across three seasons: summer, monsoon, and winter. One interesting example was explained as increasing hotness in the early morning in 2015. In 2000, it was not much away. We had "why". Still, we could not properly answer but now we know climate change.

As supplementary, they opined temperature rising annually and increasing warming days. Its evidence was dryness of cultivated land due to which the land was in-depth and multiple scratches. Therefore, we could not dig out to prepare the land for crop cultivation. As a result, we left the land barren where the irrigation system was based on monsoon rainfall and we preferred the land having canal irrigation infrastructure, although its water level was not sufficient as required because of decreasing water level of rivers, lakes, and ponds within these catchment areas. Thus, we had adverse effects on our livelihood survival and security. In the case of clean drinking water, there were disappearing water sources. It was not in 2000.

Surprisingly, they shared a story of mosquitoes. Mosquito is found at higher temperatures. In Nepal, the mosquito was found only in the Terai belt (lower altitude landscapes). In 2000, they could not have such experience. In 2015, they found at high altitude places of Surkhet (Gadhi, Kunathari, and Lekhagaon) on the third floor. It means the growth of temperature all over the year in these high-altitude places.

In case of rainfall, table 7 shows changing rainfall in the catchment areas of the Sot Khola sub-water basin experienced by the local community. In FGD and KII, the local community told their extreme experience and intense nature of monsoon only in the patch areas for 3 days long from May 28 to June 21(Jestha 15 to Asad 7) in Gadhi, Kunathari, and Lekhagaon in 2015. Such a situation was not found in 2000. In the case of monsoon rainfall, they explained that monsoon rainfall became shorter with high intensity in the watershed catchment areas (Gadhi, Lekhagaon, and Kunathari). Monsoon rainfall could not supply water as required to the local community but was disastrous to agriculture and household. Its example was the heavy rainfall of Surkhet in 2014. It induced extreme water deficit or drought in which farmers had not to have more choices in the selection of crops. There were only traditional crops having malnutrition problems induced lower productivity.   There was an irrigation problem. There was identified crop loss, diseases, insects, lower productivity, and left to the land barren. Its negative consequence was more than 3 months of food insecurity and loss of household income. In addition, the monsoon cycle was on time in 2000. However, it started late in 2015. Its result was adverse effects on the crop cycle and its productivity. They had a bad feeling of late and extended monsoon in which they told that they could not reach the right decision on paddy cultivation and harvesting. Furthermore, paddy was attacked by known and unknown insects. Thus, paddy production was adversely affected.

About snow falling, the community was excited to share their experience with snow falling not only one day but also three days in 2000. They explained how they played snows with children. However, they told now no snow was falling. Due to the increasing temperature in the winter season, snow falling has disappeared, although Gadhi, Lekhagaon, and Kunathari have higher altitudes in Surkhet.

Climate change has made critical life to biodiversity: plants and wildlife. Similar observation and sharing were found in FGD and KII in Surkhet in 2015. Without specific plants extinction, they opined general experience of extinction of local plants and local wild animals in these catchment areas in 2015. They explained local plants and animals needed a mixed climatic environment for their survival and food. Increasing temperature and decreasing rainfall have not been nutritious to local plants. At first, local plants extinct, and then wildlife migrated somewhere nutritious foods were available.

As supplementary, drought could be observed in Surkhet. It is nothing, except the growth of the water deficit. In the water deficit, water sources disappeared in the periphery of the village and walked to explore water sources far from the village. As a result, the household had to allocate more time to porter water jars from the far places in 2015. Women and children were more vulnerable to walk more instead of income-generating activities. Thus, household lost their income opportunity. Similarly, extreme rainfall-induced two major disasters: floods and landslides. Its evidence is the flood and landslide of 2014.

**RESULT AND DISCUSSION**

The above results of descriptive statistics and trend analysis provide sufficient empirical evidence and qualitative information about the variation of climatic variables: mean annual temperature and mean annual rainfall of overall Nepal, specifically Surkhet (Sot Khola sub water basin and catchment areas: Gadhi, Lekhagaon, and Kunathari). The mean annual temperature rising is

$5.27^0$C but decreasing mean annual rainfall is 391.2 mm over the last 40 years. Trend analysis shows $0.12^0$C incremental mean annual temperature per annum and 0.16 mm decremental mean annual rainfall per annum. Therefore, climate change is emerging slowly and gradually in Nepal. Its specific similar scenario is catching gradually and steadily in Surkhet.

In Nepal, climate change spreads all over the country across different altitudes and landscapes. This transboundary issue is caused by extraterritorial and territorial drivers. The extraterritorial driver is excessively GHG emission of industrial countries particularly G20 in which USA (30 %), USSR (30%), and China (10%) have predominated. In the case of territorial drivers, the nominal GHG emission of Nepal is caused by the agriculture, forest, and urbanization process. The agriculture sector excessively uses chemical fertilizer, along with livestock farming. In the forest, fire and deforestation are major causes. At a minor level, the development of industrial and transportation increases fossil fuel consumption. Therefore, the climate change of Nepal is caused by extra- territorial drivers more than territorial drivers.

Like developing countries, the economic cost of climate change in Nepal has become unaccountable visibly and invisibly direct and indirect level without industrial and urban development led to the growth of fossil fuel consumption in the economic benefit of industrial countries, G20. Its instances of the growth of disaster events and massive economic losses per annum over the last 30 years in the lower economic growth rate and small economy. Its adverse effects can be seen in GDP. The question of minimization of the excessive economic cost of climate change may be a key question. It's alternative cost-effective solution may be *lobbying, negotiation, and diplomacy* at the international level and forums such as IPCC and UNFCCC, along with regionalism and sub-regionalism. It needs strong institutions, human capacity, policy and programs, and a think tank in Nepal, along with outward activities. However, Nepal has been suffering from a weak institution with poor activities, poor performance, and poor policy behavior. Therefore, it will be a critical issue to achieve the desired goal.

In the case of the territorial driver, Nepal has successfully achieved forest coverage at 40 percent under community forest management and leasehold forest management since the 1980s to provide the right and ownership of the poor people on local resources to improve their livelihood security to reduce poverty and inequality. Except for such indirect benefit to local households, they have not achieved incentives for reducing GHG emission from fire and deforestation, despite REDD and CDM. Under REDD, few community forest managements have received some extent of incentives from carbon emission reduction credit trade. It also shows the poor capacity and poor performance of community forest management and leasehold forest management to access REDD benefits. Therefore, commercial plantation and tree cycle may be cost-effective alternatives to receive direct benefit from forest conservation and preservation to improve the socio-economic level of local households. Thus, Nepal can reduce the cost of climate change with simple and innovative cost-effective methods of the tree production cycle and commercial tree plantation by landscapes and altitudes, along with livelihood security and poverty reduction.

Agriculture and livestock farming contribute methane through the utilization of chemical fertilizer. In this regard, an organic farming system should be widely and intensively promoted by ecological demand and ecosystem cycle methods. Similarly, unsustained fossil fuel consumption in the transportation and urbanization process should be transformed into a renewable and clean energy-based system by constructing a well standard black topple roads not only in urban but also in rural areas for improving connectivity, market, and supply chain. As a by-product of urbanization, solid waste contributes to GHG emissions. Therefore, its dumping method should transform into reduction, reuse, and recycling methods so that non-renewable minerals dependency of the industry will be less by 50 percent.

# Chapter Five
## CONCLUSION

Climate change in developing countries like Nepal has become an important issue of environment and ecology. More than half of the population has experienced a variation in the global temperature in the world by $0.7^0$C over the past several decades. It is followed by melting glaciers, disturbance of the monsoon cycle, flooding, drought, and cyclones. Further, a large size of population of developing countries particularly in African and Asian countries will suffer from malnutrition, food deficit, water scarcity, deaths, and diseases in the future. Thus, climate change-induced vulnerability has become a critical issue in developing countries, particularly in Asia.

Nepal has experienced a higher frequency of natural calamities (landslides, cyclones, and flooding), variability of rainfall, and average temperature rising all over the country. There is the variability of mean temperature from $0.4^0$C to $0.6^0$C. Similarly, glacial lake outburst floods (GLOF) have occurred in Dudh Khosi GLOF 1985, Tamakhosi GLOF 1991, and Dudh Khosi GLOF, 1998. The resulting flood waves destroyed the Namche hydropower plant, many bridges, and caused loss of life. Thus, climate change vulnerability and its huge damage cost of households in Nepal have been key issues with the course of development, social security, and human welfare.

Climate change vulnerability harms a household's income, livelihood security, and welfare. In Nepal, there is a mean loss of 2,000 million Nepali Rupees per annum including dead, missing, damage, loss of asset, death of livestock. For small farmers and landless farmers, poverty and inequality reduction may be complicated policy matters.

Climate change vulnerability in Nepal has been a complex and critical issue in the field of environmental economics, ecological economics, and development economics. This issue has generated serious attention and curiosity about how much climate change vulnerability occurs in different parts of the country, what are the adaptation capacity levels of households across different income and regions, and how much these adaptation behaviors either at the individual level or community level are effective. However, there is none of the literature studying household vulnerability and adaptive behavior. In this context, this study measures whether climate change vulnerability has higher intensity and huge cost, whether households across different income levels and regions have adaptation capacity, whether households' adaptation behaviors are effective to reduce climate change vulnerability.

The overall aim of this present study is to measure climate change: Status, Trend and Forecasting at South Asia, in Nepal.

This study has employed indicator and econometric approaches to measuring the above objective. Descriptive and Time Series models were employed.

This study is based on primary cum secondary data sets as a required theoretical model of climate change vulnerability index and econometric models. Primary data related to socio-economic characteristics of the household, disaster, and adaptation behavior for this study as a case study in the watershed areas of Sot Khola (Gadhi, Lekhagaon, and Kunathari) was collected through a Household survey. Its sample size was 20 percent sample household (642 households) from three VDCs as selected proportional stratified random sampling method to select sample household from 9 clusters based on different ethnic groups, income groups, and geographical locations of VDCs so that all clusters could represent proportionally in the survey.

As supplementary data and information, secondary data related to temperature, rainfall, and precipitation from 1990 to 2015 were collected from the Department of Hydrology and Meteorology, Nepal Government.

The study through the above research methods has the following findings presented concerning its objectives.

## CLIMATE CHANGE

The findings are related to the climate change of Nepal, climate change of Surkhet and watershed areas, climate change-induced multiple hazards and vulnerability.

In the climate change of Nepal, variations in temperature and rainfall are influenced by heterogeneous altitudes. Temperature variation in maximum annual in Nepal is 0.06°C a year. The maximum temperature had increased by 0.4°C, minimum temperature by 0.2°C, and the mean temperature increase by 0.7°C between 1989 and 2010.  The highest altitude has the lowest temperature and the lowest altitude has the highest temperature. It shows that the winter season is colder than before and summer is hotter than before. For the next 30 years (from 2010 to 2040), the temperature will incline to the annual growth rate of 0.4°C-0.6°C. In the rainfall structure, monsoon with 80 percent dominates to pre and post-monsoon.  Its trend is found declining. For the next 29 years, its trend line is slightly declining. Thus, climate change in the different parts of Nepal occurs. Similarly, in the climate change of the study areas, the temperature is found increasing present trend more than past 20 years.

There are found two major climate change hazards: floods and landslides. These climate changes induced hazards have resulted in different vulnerabilities and impacts on the catchment areas. Firstly, the flood of upstream to downstream has induced bank cutting of agricultural land. Its measure is 16.4 hectares in total. Its number indicates more events in Kunathari than Lekhagaon and Gadhi. Although all are vulnerable, Kunathari is more vulnerable to VDC than Lekhagaon and Gadhi. Secondly, in 2014, the landslide had 29 events creating extreme vulnerability to households more than a flood. A landslide is ranked in the first disaster and a flood is ranked in the second disaster.

Flood has bank cutting hugely, converted agricultural land into sediment land, and damaged water mills. Besides it, it damaged life and bridges. The landslide has swept to houses, terrace land, and water tanks. Kunathari lies in the first rank followed by Lekhagoan in the second rank and by Gadhi in the third rank. Flood has more impact than a landslide.

The flood and landslide of Sot Khola 2014 damaged Rs 13,344,000 houses and property loss, Rs 798,777 crops, Rs 410,000 livestock, and Rs 3, 911,650 income losses. Thus, the total loss was Rs 18,464,427. The household vulnerability was huge in terms of loss. Its distribution was different to the different geography. In Gadhi and Lekhagaon, the household vulnerability was less than in Kunathari. Agricultural income has a significant impact on household vulnerability. The early warning seemed to be more effective to reduce household vulnerability than knowledge of disaster.

Climate change Issues:

- Unstable Global, Regional, and National Trend of climate change
- Critical level of GHG emission of Industrial countries (G20) to developing countries
- Poor GHG emission reduction friendly development and governance system of developing countries
- Excessive use of chemical fertilizer and pesticide at the farm in developing countries for higher crop yield
- Growth of forest fire in a developing country, in Nepal
- Increasing unexpectedly glaciers and glacier bursting risk in climate change but receiving less priority from the world instead of coastal areas impact

- Growth of desertification of fertile land
- Destruction of landscapes without conservation
- Blindness towards a haphazard development with rampant leakages
- Magnificant frequency of climate-induced multi-hazard (heavy rainfall, low rainfall, temperature stress, desertification, soil erosion, forest fire, flood, landslide, and drought) and vulnerability
- Increasing mosquito at high altitude
- Shifting habitats of wildlife: snakes, tiger, leopard, etc
- Increasing landscape vulnerability
- No mitigation activities
- No academic discourses and no collaboration with academic and research institutions,
- Climatic data management and analysis

## ALTERNATIVE

Climatic catastrophe is Tran's boundary issues or commons of the world. Whatever format, form, and driver of this undesired climatic issue has started to affect Nepal, like South Asian countries. Its evidence is our glacier bursting and its flood in the last decade, along with increasing temperature rising stress in urban and rural areas, and decreasing water source stress in rural areas. To date, about 20 glacier lakes are at high risk. Settlements of Himal, Hill, and Terai are vulnerable more than before. Agriculture and hydro projects are mostly exposed. Thus, the natural disaster annual cycle has become faster and more disastrous than before. Let's imagine what will be the size of economic loss in the context of 2000 million Rupees' economic loss per annum. For maintaining higher economic growth, overall development dynamics, and welfare of the people, climate change stabilization if is an international issue, climate change neutralization should be initiated from top to bottom approach or from bottom to top approach. Otherwise, the climatic disaster cycle may derail serverly higher economic growth, overall development dynamics, and welfare of the people. Therefore, the following alternatives as vision based on the above results are presented below for its in-depth, scientific, and analytical discourse.

Alternative: *Go Green Economy*

> *Go Green Economy* is not a new approach in the world. This approach is widely popular. To some extent, G20 countries have adopted this approach beyond the limit of economic growth for sustainable economic growth and development. In the case of developing countries, higher economic growth is a target of their development efforts to follow such developed countries' growth model in which governance, institution, and market are perfect

and efficient. In developing countries, they do have not such a level of resource efficiency and effectiveness. In this context, the developing countries should exhaust excessively resources, time, and effort to have a better result from such a growth model. Therefore, developing countries follow their natural resource and their conservation-based development model by using cost-effective and innovative technology and knowledge. Thus, developing countries will get the fruit of go green economy from production, consumption and distribution, and international trade.

To go fully green economy, developing countries should modify with the following reforms in the present development policy and model as follows.

Output I: *Go Green Output, Production, and Consumption*

*Activity I: Landscape Conservation and Preservation*

It must be. Its basic idea is landscape is correlated with climate and climate-induced multiple natural hazards. Its violation that includes forest fire, land changes, etc. generates carbon footprints. In recent years, haphazard local development that is so-called *excavator development* is done by *excavator* drivers where they think a need for road development and other infrastructure. Traditionally, parental property right is on land. Its result is land fragmentation into small pieces. In urban areas, the buffer zone of the river, conservation, road, drinking water, and hydro projects are not protected. Its result is encroachment. All these activities are carbon emission friendly. Therefore, landscape reform policy should be initiated to conserve and preserve the landscape in which in agriculture, land should be categorized into fertile and non-fertile land. Fertile land should be conserved by giving output divisible property right in agriculture. Nonfertile land should be allocated for infrastructure and settlement. All infrastructures should be developed buffer zone for controlling encroachment for minimizing disaster loss.

*Activity II: Clean Energy*

Energy is a must to improve economic production activities and household livelihood and welfare. It facilitates multiple options for production activities. For example: if the village has a water shortage, energy facilitates the villager to use a water turbine for water lifting from rivers and lakes. If energy is not available, such an option will not be used. Therefore, energy is an inevitable variable in the household economy and sectoral economy for operation, management, and productivity. In Nepal, hydro has a huge prospect. Therefore, multi-purpose hydro projects should be developed at the macro and the micro-level. Due to climate change, we cannot predict its future after the next 50 years. As an alternative, Nepal should move simultaneously a big solar energy harvesting projects in Hill regions where sunlight is comfortable feasible. Only this source will be valuable to clean energy for going green.

It is not sufficient only intervention in production side but consumption side should be encouraged to clean energy. Consumer behavior should *go green economy* friendly that is clean energy-based cooking, heating, and lighting system and using efficient cooking, heating, and lighting equipment. In addition, transportation should be in either electric or clean energy. Thus, GHG emissions will be mitigated.

*Activity III: Production, Consumption, and Distribution of Green Products*

How can we achieve a higher economic growth rate if we talk about the transformation of manufacturing industries, although agriculture, green, and service products dominate in production, consumption, and distribution in developing countries, and what would be tradeable products are key issues? In Nepal, manufacturing industries are feasible in terms of agricultural products. Otherwise, it would not feasible if we give a logic of comparative benefit of labor only. Its pace will not be sustainable because industrial development requires doing business environment, discipline skill labor and enterprises culture. Why do we prefer such a sector which will not carry out miracles and revolutionary? In this context, what will be an alternative? In recent years, the world talks about going green. It will be relevant.

- In general, capacity leads to prospects. In the manufacturing sector, we have to develop. Its cost is huge. If we follow, it may be fake and an illusion over time. In agriculture, we have the required capacity. I holistically and intuitively only find a great prospect within a limited time, like as green revolution. At present, chemicals and pesticides have severely damaged soil fertility and productivity of agriculture. It is also the source of GHG emissions and stabilizes climate change. If we focus on environmentally friendly farming, we can reduce its cost of production based on soil fertility, natural productivity, and cost-reducing benefit in our livelihood. Of course, it will not be fast but will be sustainable not only production but also consumption and healthy and happy life. Another implication can be found in declining GHG emission and improving climate change stability and minimizing climate change disasters. Despite the growth of the population, we can yield sufficient healthy and nutritious foods. It means what. Its output will be healthy, happy, and creative life having expanding expectations of life and a higher fertility rate over a long period. At lower natural catastrophe, soil fertility and assets loss will be minima. It means no more money for infrastructure and assets. Thus, consumption and distribution will be organic products at a lower price. Daily livelihood cost will be the least. Thus, life will be zero stress. It will be a great revolutionary.

- In the service sector, education, health, IT, and research servicing should be focused. It is not easy at present to western module service sector infrastructure and human resources in developing countries because of low comparative benefit in terms of infrastructure, schooling, skilled manpower, and approach. In this present situation, we have a higher probability if developing countries have either talented people or a similar level of approach, institution, and policy. However, the imperfection from politics to economics and social structure is a constraint. Therefore, the products and services of developed countries have dominated developing countries.

Its alternative is the revival of eastern ideas and knowledge in the service sector including education and health, along with western education and health.

Output II: Infrastructure Development and Capacity Building

*Activity I: Institutional Development-Climate Change Fund, Climate Change Forum, and Climate Research Center, Rescue, Recovery and Rehabilitation Center*

Despite informal institutions, we need institutions related to the green economy. Maybe, we have in function but not at the optimal level. Maybe, we do have not as required function, structure, network, and format of the institution to our national and local level green dreams. Our key concern is to establish the green system, to promote information, technology, and knowledge, and to forward such lessons on the management of climate change disasters (rescue, recovery, and rehabilitation).

In the case of existing institutions and systems, the government should reform radically and fastly towards the green economy. In the case of a new institution and system, the government should establish a new institution as required to our green economy. Its functional approach should be an integrity approach related to output-oriented activities and system building.

*Activity II: Development of Innovative Technology and Production, Consumption and Distribution*

Technology makes the world smart and efficient in production, consumption, and distribution. In the case of a green economy, green-friendly innovative technology should be discovered in production, consumption, and distribution to extend its capacity to a large scale. It is possible only when science and technology are well developed through innovative research centers and scientists. In production, technology should be green fuel-friendly with high efficiency, like in consumption. Transportation technology should be green fuel and clean energy-friendly. Therefore, science and technology should be developed in the country.

*Activity Output III: Green Friendly Financial Management and Trade*

Trade is vital to drive production, consumption, and distribution. For it, financial management and system should be green-friendly to promote trade flow.

Output III: Mitigation and Adaptation

Disaster is a natural phenomenon having uncertain and paradoxical cycles due to the composition and decomposition of natural elements and changing structures of landscape, hydrology, metrology, forest, etc. Maybe it would be least its coverage, frequency, intensity, and strength. However, disaster will be. Therefore, the following activity should be promoted.

*Activity I: Preparedness-Climate Change Capacity Building and Awareness Campaign*

*Activity II: Satellite and International organization based Climatic Alert system*

*Activity III: Plantation and Forest Conservation*

# REFERENCES


Acharya, S. P. (2012). Is climate change engulfing Nepal faster? *Mirmire (English Edition).* 40 (312), 5.

Acharya, S. P., and Bhatta, G.R. (2013). *The impact of climate change on agricultural growth in Nepal.* Working paper series, 15(201).

ADB (2018) *Assessing the Costs of Climate Change and Adaptation in South Asia, http:// www.adb.org/Assessing the Costs of Climate Change and Adaptation in South Asia*

Adger, W. N (2006). Vulnerability. *Global Environmental Change,* 16 (3), 268-281.

Adger, WN. (1999). Social vulnerability to climate change and extremes in coastal Vietnam. *World Development,* 27, 249-269.

Ahmed, M. & Supachalasai, S.(2014). *Assessing the costs of climate change and adaptation in South Asia.* Philippines: ADB

Aryal, J.P., Sapkota, T.B., Khurana, R. , *et al.* Climate change and agriculture in South Asia: adaptation options in smallholder production systems. *Environ Dev Sustain* **22,** 5045–5075 (2020). https://doi.org/10.1007/s10668-019-00414-4

Basnet, K. (1989). Temperature Variation in Nepal. *Himalayan Review, 20*, 25-34. Retrieved from https://www.nepjol.info/index.php/HR/article/view/2409

BehrenW., Randers, J., Meadows, D. and Meadow, D. (1972). *The limit to growth*. New York: A Potomac Associates Book.

Bhandari, G. (2013). Effect of precipitation and temperature variation on the yield of major cereals in Dedeldhura Districts of Far Western Development Region, Nepal. *International Journal of Plant, Animal and Environmental Sciences*, 3(1), Jan- Mar.

Brooks, N., Adger, W. and Mick Kelly, P. (2005). The determinants of vulnerability and adaptive capacity at the national level and the implications for adaptation. *Global Environmental Change*, Part A 15, 151-163.

Central Bureau of Statistics (CBS). (1991). *Population census*. Kathmandu: CBS

Central Bureau of Statistics (CBS). (2011). *Population census*. Kathmandu: CBS

Central Bureau of Statistics (CBS). (2017). *Environmental Statistics*. Kathmandu: CBS

Chalise, S.R and Khanal, N.R. (2002) 'Recent extreme weather events in the Nepal Himalayas'. In Snorasson, A.; Finnsdottir, H.P.; Moss, M.E. (eds) *The extremes of the extremes: Extraordinary floods*, Publication 271, 141-146. Reykjavik (Iceland): IAHS

Cutter, Susan L. 2003. The vulnerability of science and the science of vulnerability. *Annals of the Association of American Geographers* 93 (1), 1-12.

Dahal, R.K., Hasegawa, S., Nonomura, A., Yamanaka, M., Dhakal, S., and Paudyal, P. (2008). Predictive modeling of rainfall-induced landslide hazard in the Lesser Himalaya of Nepal based on weights-of-evidence. *Geomorphology, 102*, 496–510.

DDC (District Development Committee) (2015). *District Profile.* Surkhet: DDC

DHM(Department of Hydrology and Metrology), (2019). *Temperature report.* Kathmandu: DHM

Easter, C. (1999). Small states development: A Commonwealth vulnerability index. *The Round Table, 351,*403-422.

Elisch, J. (2008). *Climate change: Financing global forests.* London: The Stationery Office Limited.

Ford, J. and Smit, B. (2004). A Framework for Assessing the Vulnerability of Communities in the Canadian Arctic to Risks. *Journal of Climate Change.* 57(4), 389– 400.

Füssel H-M (2004) Coevolution of the political and conceptual frameworks for climate change vulnerability assessments. In: Biermann F, Campe S, Jacob K (eds) Proceedings of the 2002 Berlin conference on the human dimensions of global environmental change "Knowledge for the Sustainability Transition. The Challenge for Social Science". Global Governance Project, Amsterdam, The Netherlands, pp 326–344.

Fussel, H.M. (2007). Vulnerability: A generally applicable conceptual framework for climate change research. *Global Environmental Change,* 17, 155–167.

Füssel, H-M. and Klein, R.J. (2003). Vulnerability and adaptation assessments to climate change: An evolution of conceptual thinking' Paper presented at UNDP Expert Group Meeting *Integrating disaster reduction and adaptation to climate change*, Havana, Cuba, 17-19 June 2002.

Government of Nepal (GON)(2014). *Factsheet of Disaster*. Kathmandu: GON

Hanif Uzma, Syed, S.H., Ahmad, R., and Malik, K.A. (2010). *The economic impact of climate change on the agricultural sector of Punjab,* publication in 2009 retrieved from http://www.pide.org.pk/psde/25/pdf/agm26/day3/Uzma%20Hanif.pdf.

Hansen, J., Sato, M. and Ruedy, R. (2011). *Climate variability and climate change: The New climate dice.* New York: The Goddard Institute for Space Studies (GISS).

Hare, F.R.(1953). *The Restless Atmosphere.* London: Hutchinson University Library.

Hassan, R. (2008). Implications of climate change for agricultural sector performance in Africa: Policy challenges and research agenda. *Journal of African Economics* 19(2): 77-105.

IPCC(Intergovernmental Panel on Climate Change), (1990). *Climate Change: The IPCC1990.* Cambridge: Cambridge University Press.

IPCC(Intergovernmental Panel on Climate Change), (1995). *IPCC Second Assessment Report.* Cambridge: Cambridge University Press.

IPCC(Intergovernmental Panel on Climate Change), (2001). *TAR Climate Change 2001: the scientific basis.* Cambridge: Cambridge University Press.

IPCC(Intergovernmental Panel on Climate Change), (2007). *Working Group II Summary for Policy Makers.* Cambridge: Cambridge University Press.

IPCC (Intergovernmental Panel on Climate Change), (2008) *Climate Change and Water.* Cambridge: Cambridge University Press.

Joshi, G.R. and Thapa, S. (2010). A Ricardian analysis of the climate change impact on Nepalese agriculture. Paper submitted to *International*

*Conference of Biodiversity, Livelihood and Climate Change* in the Himalayas12-14 December 2010, Kathmandu, Nepal

K.C., S. (2013). Community vulnerability to floods and landslides in Nepal. *Ecology and Society* 18(1), 8,

Kaly, U and Pratt, C. (2000). *Environmental vulnerability index: Development and provisional indices and profiles for Fiji, Samoa, Tuvalu, and Vanuatu.* Phase II report for NZODA. SOPAC Technical Report 306, 89.

Kaly, U; Briguglio, L; McLeod, H; Schmall, S; Pratt, C; and R Pal. (1999). Environmental vulnerability index (EVI) to summarize national environmental vulnerability profiles. *SOPAC Technical Report, 275,* 66.

Kamanou, G. and Morduch, J. (2005). Measuring vulnerability to poverty, in: Dercon, S. (Ed.), *Insurance against poverty.* London: Oxford University Press.

Karki M. B, Shrestha A.B., Winiger M. (2011). Enhancing knowledge management and adaptation capacity for integrated management of water resources in the Indus River Basin. *Mountain Research and Development* 31(3):242–251.

Karn, P.K.(2014). *The impact of climate change on rice production in Nepal.* SANDEE Working Paper No. 85-14. Kathmandu: SANDEE

Kurukulasuriya, P. and Ajwad, M.(2004). Estimating the impact of climate change on smallholders: A case study on the agricultural sector in Sri Lanka. In Mendelsohn R et al. (eds), Cross-Sectional Analyses of Climate Change Impacts. *World Bank Policy Research Working Paper No. 3350.*

Malla, G. (2008). Climate change and impact on Nepalese agriculture. *Journal of Agriculture and Environment,* 9(5).

Mendelsohn, R., W. Nordhaus, and D. Shaw.(1994). The impact of global warming on agriculture: A Ricardian analysis. *American Economic Review*, 84,753-771.

Mirza Nomman, A and Schmitz, P.M. (2011).Using the Ricardian Technique to estimate the impact of Climate change on crop farming in Pakistan paper prepared for presentation at the *EAAE 2011 Congress*, Switzerland.

Mool, PK; Bajracharya, SR; Joshi, SP (2001a) Inventory of glaciers, glacial lakes, and glacial lake outburst floods: Monitoring and early warning systems in the Hindu Kush-Himalayan region – Nepal. Kathmandu: ICIMOD

Morrow, B.H. (1999). Identifying and mapping community vulnerability. *Disasters,* 23, 1–18.

Moss R.H., Brenkert, A.L. and Malone, E.L. (2001). *Vulnerability to climate change: A Quantitative Approach.* Washington DC: Department of Energy.

Nicholls, R.J., Leatherman, S.P, Dennis, K.C. and Volonte, C. R. (1995). Impacts and responses to sea-level rise: Qualitative and quantitative assessments. *Journal of Coastal Research,* 14, 26-43.

O'Brien, K., Leichenko, R., Kelkar, U., Venema, H., Aandahl, G., Tompkins, H., Javed, A., Bhadwal, S., Barg, S., and Nygaard, L. (2004). Mapping vulnerability to multiple stressors: climate change and globalization in India. *Global Environmental Change* Part A 14, 303-313.

Oliver, J.E. & Hidoc, J.J, (1984). Climatology-An introductions. New York: Bell and Howell

Owen, A and Hanley, N (eds) (2004) *The economics of climate change.* London: Taylor and Francis Group.

Pant, K.P. (2011). Economics of climate change for smallholder farmers in Nepal: A Review paper, *The Journal of Agricultural and Environment*, 12(5).

Pant, K.P. (2012). Climate change and food security in Nepal. *The Journal of Agricultural and Environment*, 13(5).

Parry, M.L., Canziani, O.F., Palutikof, J.P., van der Linden, P.J. and Hanson, C.E. (2007). *Contribution of working group II to the fourth assessment report of the intergovernmental panel on climate change.* London: Cambridge University Press.

Patnaik, U and Narayanan, K. (2005). *Vulnerability and climate change: An analysis of the Eastern Coastal Districts of India*, Human Security, and Climate Change: An International Workshop, Asker.

Ramos-Martin, J(2001a). Historical analysis of energy intensity of Spain: From a conventional view to an integrated assessment. *Population and Environment, 22(3):281-313.*

Ravindranath, N. and Sathaye, J (2003). *Climate change and developing countries.* New York: Kluwer Academic Publishers

Salinger, M. J. (2005). *Climate variability and change: Past, present, and future – An overview.* Hamilton: National Institute of Water and Atmospheric Research.

Seo, N. and R. Mendelsohn. (2008). A Ricardian analysis of the Impact of climate change on South American farms. *Chilean Journal of Agricultural Research,* 68(1), 69-79.

Seo, N.S., R. Mendelsohn, A. Dinar, R. Hassan, and P.Kurukulasuriya (2009). A Ricardian analysis of the distribution of climate change impacts on agriculture across agro-ecological zones in Africa. *Environmental Resource Economics,* 43, 313-332.

Shrestha, S.L., Maharjan, K.L., and Joshi, N.P. (2012). Relationship between Climate Variables and Yields of Food crops in Nepal: Cases of Makwanpur and Ilam Districts. *Journal of International Development and Cooperation,* 18(4), 37- 54.

Sterns, N. (2006). *The Economics of Climate Change.* London: H.M Treasury.

Sterns, N. (2007). *The Economics of Climate Change.* London: H.M Treasury.

United Nations (UN)(2019). *UN news.* Washington: UN

United Nations Framework Conventions on Climate Change (UNFCCC). (2002a). *Climate change: Impacts, vulnerabilities, and adaptation in developing countries.* Bonn: UNFCCC Secretariat.

United Nations Framework Conventions on Climate Change (UNFCCC). (2008). *Climate change: Impacts, vulnerabilities, and adaptation in developing countries.* Bonn: UNFCCC Secretariat.

United States Geological Survey (USGS) (2007). *Climate variability and change: Facing tomorrow's challenges-USGS Science in the Decade 2007-2017,* Publication in 2006 retrieved from http://pubs.er.usgs.gov/usgspubs/cir/cir1309

Va´squez-Leo´ n, M., West, C.T., Finan, T.J., (2003). A comparative assessment of climate vulnerability: agriculture and ranching on both sides of the US–Mexico border. *Global Environmental Change* 13, 159–173.

Vincent, K. (2004). *Creating an index of social vulnerability to climate change in Africa.* UK: Tyndall Centre for Climate Change Research. Publication in 2003 retrieved from http://www.tyndall.ac.uk/publications/working_papers/wp56.pdf

Watkiss, P., D. Anthoff, T. Downing, C. Hepburn, C. Hope, A. Hunt and R. Tol, (2005). The social costs of carbon (SCC) review: Methodological approaches for using SCC estimates in policy assessment, *Final*

*Report*. London: Department for Environment, Food and Rural Affairs (Defra) retrieved from http://www.defra.gov.uk/environment/climatechange/research/carboncost/pdf/ aeat-scc-report.pdf.

WB(World Bank), (2009). *Why is South Asia Vulnerable to Climate Change?* http://go.worldbank.org/OJ4FWPUB10

# ANNEX I: STUDY AREA

The selection of Surkhet District (Figure 29) had reasons as follows: (a) DHM data sets of this district showed changing climate variables including temperature, precipitation, and rainfall in the range from the valley to the Mahabharata by the hydrological and topographical department; (b) this district was the highly vulnerable area from the aspects of natural hazard like as flooding and landslide, along with changing climate variables; (c) this district had a variation of ecology and topography for comparative aspects; (d) the district has Sot Khola sub river basin carrying natural disaster in the periphery areas of the river basin; and (e) the Sot Khola sub river basin was a virgin area for the study and its outputs would be valuable for policy intervention to the policymaker (DHM, 2015, DDC, 2015 and Field Survey, 2015).

## SOT KHOLA: ECOLOGICAL BELT, DISTRICT AREA AND LOCATION OF RIVERS

Surkhet is a district unit located 600 kilometers west of Kathmandu valley (the details in Figure 2). It lies in the Bheri Zone of the Mid-Western Development region (DDC, 2015). Its size is approximately 2,451 km$^2$ lying between the latitude of 28°20' N to 28°58' N and longitude 80°59' E to 82°02'E. Its district borders are Dang and Salyan in the east; Doti, Achham, and Kailali in the west; Dailekh and Jajarkot in the north; and Baradiya and Banke in the south (the details in Figure 2). Birendranagar is her headquarter at 680-meters altitude from sea level. Geologically, the valley was a lake before thousand years ago (DDC, 2015).

In Surkhet, the total population is about 350 thousand, in which the sex ratio is 0.92 with 52 percent females (CBS, 2011). Out of the total population, the poverty level is 30 percent. Its rank is at 49th with 36.4 values in HPI. HDI 2014 ranks the district at 34th with 0.476 values. The income per capita of the district is 563 USD that is lower than 718 USD of the national average (DDC, 2015). There is heterogeneous castes including Chhetri, Brahmin, Janajati, Dalit, Thakuri, and the minority castes (Tharu, Badi, Newar & Muslim). In the caste distribution, Chhetri dominates with 32 percent to all. Dalit (25 percent) and minority castes (20 percent) follow it.

The district is categorized into the weak landscapes because the district is dominated by 57 percent rugged hilly land. It is followed by 42 percent plain land. In the rugged hilly land, there are 15 percent Siwalika and 43 percent Mahabharata Range. Out of 57 percent, hilly land, its 18 percent landscapes are $90^0C$ vertical topography in which nothing can be done, except conservation. Its topographical distribution is as follows in Table -2.

Despite the weak landscape of the district, it is agrarian. Out of 42 percent plain total land, approximately 25 percent land is employed for agricultural activity. In agriculture, there are the following patterns of crops: major crops (paddy, wheat, and maize) and non-traditional crops (vegetables, citrus fruits, potato, mustard, and lentils). However, food security is still critical because of low productivity. Low productivity is due to year-round irrigation to one-third of cultivated lands.

The ecology varies across different altitudes from 198 meters to 2367 meters from sea level. Climate zones are four in Surkhet (DDC, 2015) (Table 8). There are hot and dry sub-tropics to cool temperate. Mean temperature ranges from $4.5^0C$ min. to $37.1^0C$ max. Mean rainfall is 1603 mm. In monsoon, rainfall is recorded at 1312 mm.

**Table 8: Ecological Elevation**

| Climate Zone | Elevation Range (Meter) | Percent of area (%) |
| --- | --- | --- |
| Lower Tropical | Below 300 | 2.2 |
| Upper Tropical | 300-1000 | 61.9 |
| Sub-Tropical | 1000 to 2000 | 32.8 |
| Temperate | 2000 to 3000 | 1.3 |

Source: *CBS, 2015*

Surkhet is rich in natural resources. A large area is covered by forest (71.4%) and agriculture plus settlement (26.4%). In addition, it is rich in water resources including Bheri and Karnali as major rivers and Chigadh Khola, Jhupra Khola, Simta Khola, Jum Khola, Rate Khola, Khakhre Khola, Gam Khola, Guthu Khola, Soth Khola, Goche Khola, Neware Khola, Itram Khola, Khorke Khola, Girighat Khola, Bidhyapur Khola, etc. as minor rivers (DDC, 2015). Its topographic distribution is in Table 9.

**Table 9: Topography Distribution**

| S.N. | Topography (Degree) | Altitude Category (Meter) | Percentage (%) |
| --- | --- | --- | --- |
| 1 | <3 | 121.50 | 0.05 |
| 2 | 3-15 | 137.79 | 5.83 |
| 3 | 15-30 | 1111.02 | 44.62 |
| 4 | 30-66 | 2490.16 | 49.50 |
|  | Total | 3740.19 | 100 |

Source: *CBS, 2015*

# STUDY AREA: SOT KHOLA WATER BASIN AND CATCHEMNT AREA

**Figure 13: Study Area (Sot Khola sub water basin and catchment area)**

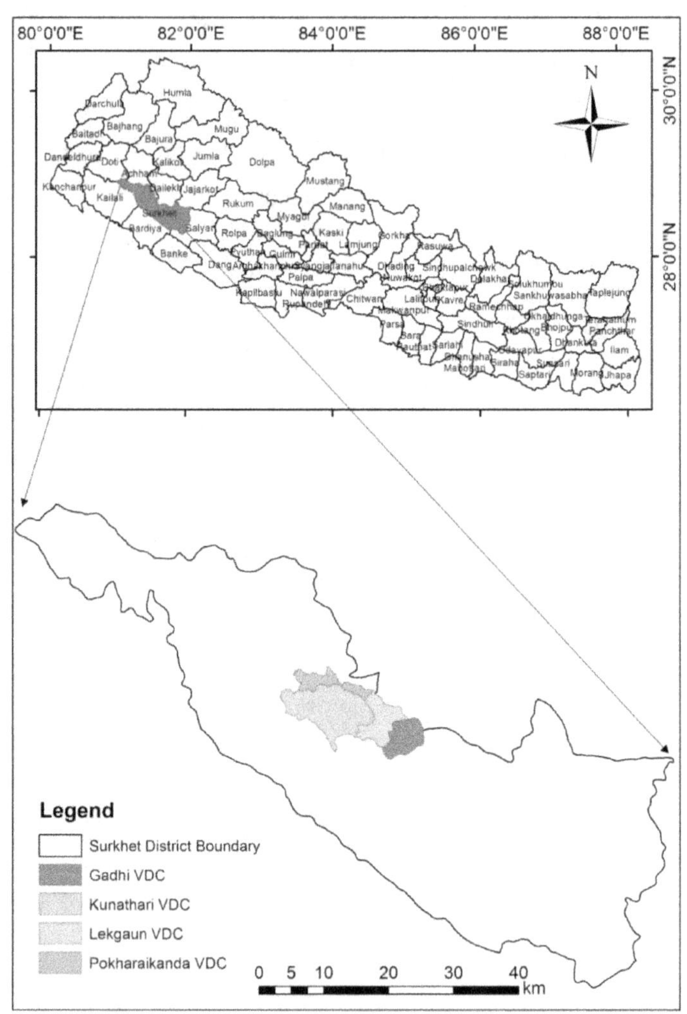
"

**Figure 14: Sot Khola Catchment Areas**

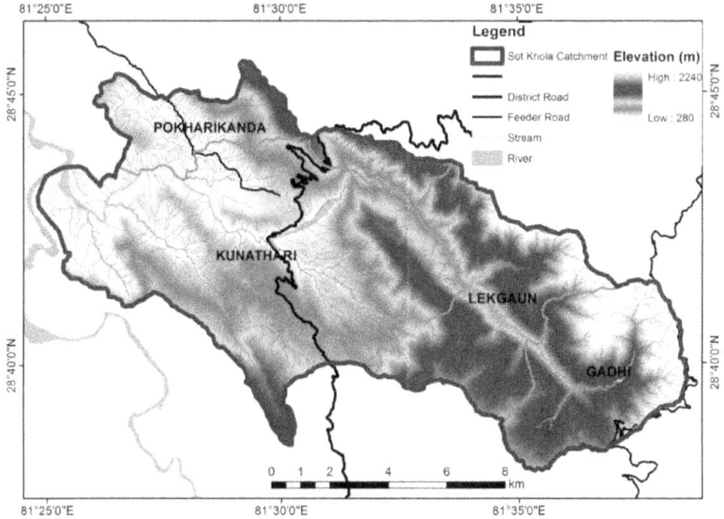

Sot Khola is one of the important sub-water basins (Figure-13 and Figure-14). Its upstream area is Chandane, Gadhi VDC and its downstream is Rakseni, Kunathari VDC (Figure-29 and Figure-30). Its catchment areas are three VDCs namely Gadhi (Upper stream), Lekhagaon (middle stream), and Kunathari (downstream) (DDC, 2015) (the details in Annex IX). The Sot Khola is one of the tributaries of the Bheri River (Figure-29). Its length is about 30 km (DDC, 2015).

Its catchment areas are as follows.

a)  Gadhi VDC is the catchment area of the Sot Khola sub-water basin at the altitude of 1200 meters in the Mahabharata Range (Figure-13 and Figure-14) (the details in Annex III). Its location is 9 km far north from District headquarter.  Its area is 28 square km. Population size is 3369 out of which main castes are Magar (37.7 percent), Brahmin (30.6 percent), Chhetri (17.1

percent), Sunwar (5.7 percent), and others (22.6 percent). Others include Kami, Sarki, Thakuri, Gurung, Damai, Sherpa, etc. (VDC, 2015).

b) Lekhgaon VDC is another catchment VDC lying 198 meters (Tata pani) to 2369 meters (Matela gurase) altitude (Figure-13 and Figure-14) (the details in Annex VIII). It spreads 110 km length and 30 km breadth of 2451 sq. km (249,016 hectares) (the details in Annex-III). Hill dominates with 84 percent. The remaining 16 percent is the valley. Population size is 3999 (651 households) (DDC, 2015).

c) Kunathari is a catchment area lying between 600 meters and 1200 meters (Figure-13 and Figure-14) (the details in Annex III). It is 20 km far from the district headquarter (the details in Annex-III). Population size is 3413 (CBS, 1991) and (DDC, 2015).

## ANNEX II: METHOD OF STUDY

### Conceptual Approach

IPCC Third Assessment Report (2001) states that vulnerability is a function of the character, magnitude, and rate of climate variation to which a system is exposed its sensitivity and its adaptive capacity. This is a theoretical concept of vulnerability.

Let us suppose vulnerability of any region (i) as dependent variable (V) and climate hazard (H) sensitivity (S), and adaptive capacity (A) as independent variables. Mathematically, there is a functional relationship between vulnerability (V), climate hazard (H), sensitivity (S), and adaptive capacity (A). It can be expressed as follows:

$$V_i = f (H_i, S_i, A_i) \dots\dots\dots (1)$$

Where,

Climatic Hazard ($H_i$) includes sub-variables such as flood, drought, landslide, cyclone, etc. after the occurrence of climate variability in the i[th] region. Such hazards are sensitive to humans and the environment. Present and future damages of climatic hazards can be minimized by adaptive capacity (A). Adaptive Capacity is comprised of socio-economic capacity, technology access, and infrastructure.

Fussel (2004) provides the conceptual framework in which four variables: (i) the system (or region and/or population group and/or sector) and (ii) the hazard (or threats or stressors) (iii) the consequences (or effects of climate change), and (iv) a temporal reference (time frame), are mentioned.

**Analytical Framework**

Ford and Smit (2004) developed this analytical framework based on IPCC theoretical framework (Figure 15). This tool assesses climate change vulnerability levels not only at present but also at the future.

**Figure 15: Analytical Framework for Vulnerability Assessment**

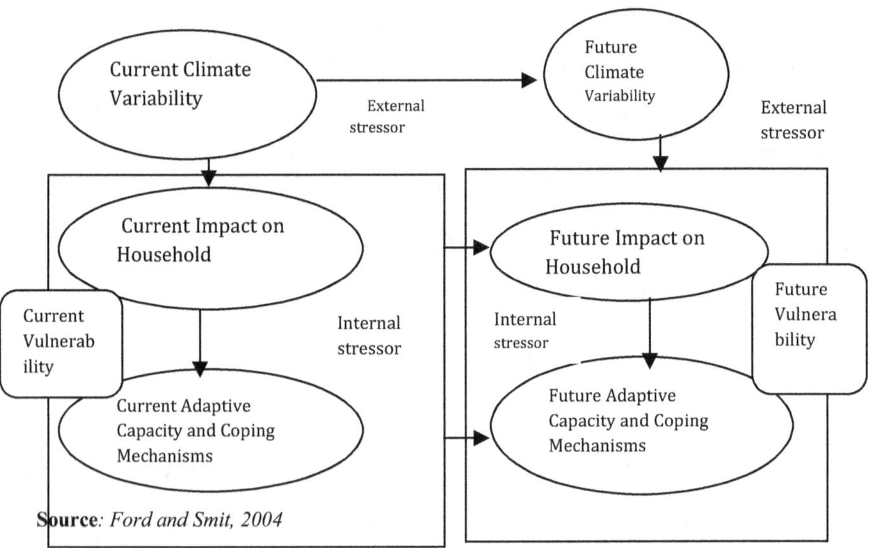


*Source: Ford and Smit, 2004*

Ford and Smit (2004) explain about two levels (Figure 4). The first level measures current vulnerability based on three variables such as current climatic hazard and current adaptive capacity and coping mechanisms. Climatic hazard contains damages to the household by flood, landslide, and cyclones. Household adaptive capacity at the individual and at the collective level has consisted of indigenous knowledge and technology and socio-economic capacity. This capacity can lessen biophysical damages to the household. Then, current vulnerability can be measured. Similarly, the second level measures future vulnerability based on the assumption that climate variability with human activity-induced GHG emission stock and growth results in future climatic hazard to households and future adaptive capacity and mechanisms. This capacity will be an innovation of technology and infrastructure development to reduce biophysical damages to households, along with public intervention. Then, future vulnerability can be measured.

## MODEL

### Theoretical model for Objective 1

The theoretical model of this study(Figure 16) is based on a simple regression model to describe possible relationships between variables. The tool is used to explain the trend line of temperature and rainfall for understanding its long movement by using time series data of temperature and rainfall. It finds variations on whether a particular data set of temperature and rainfall have increased or decreased over

**Figure 16: Indicator & Index Method**

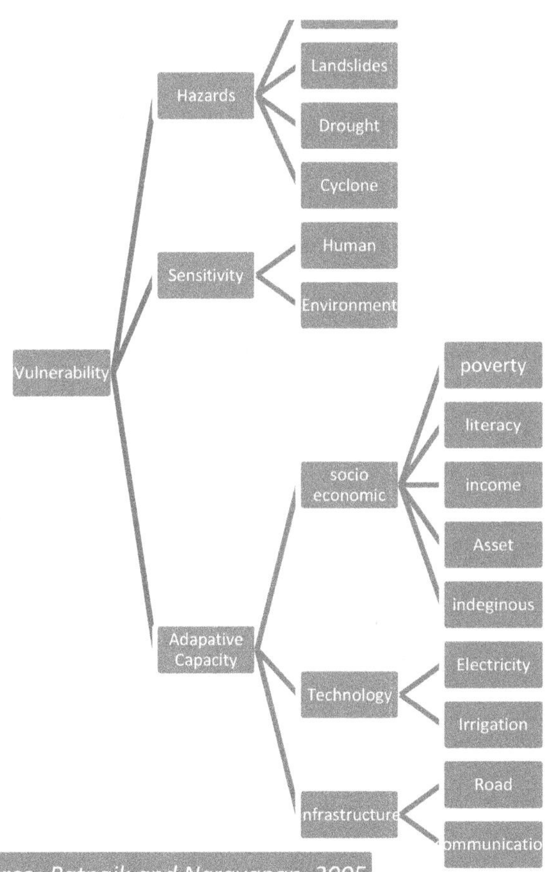

time. In addition, it forecasts temperature and rainfall variation and pattern in the coming time based on its observed data sets.

**Approach and method of climate change vulnerability for objective 2**

There are two types of analytical methods to measure climate change vulnerability. They are the indicator approach and econometric approach.

**Indicator Approach**

This approach that is quantitative assessment is widely used by Brooks et al. (2005), Cutter et al. (2003), Easter (1999), Kaly et al. (1999), Kaly and Pratt (2000). The selected indicators may be used at the local (Adger 1999; Morrow 1999 and Vasquez et al. 2003;), national (O'Brien et al. 2004), regional (Leichenko and O'Brien, 2001 and Vincent, 2004), or global (Brooks et al. 2005 and Moss et al. 2001) scales. This approach is based on a wide range of indicators. These indicators, which are scaled up for measuring vulnerability are used to develop a vulnerability index of the system or place or population.  The index provides the intensity of vulnerability.

**Indicators and Index Method**

In the construction of the index, indicators are inevitable elements (the details in Figure-15 and Figure-16). These indicators are presented and arranged into socioeconomic, demographic, agricultural, occupational, climatic, geographic, etc., as Patnaik and Narayanan (2005).

Socioeconomic

- Income
- Asset
- Poverty

Demographic

- Density of population
- Literacy rate
- Mortality rate

Agricultural

- Forest area
- Production
- Crop intensity
- Irrigation
- Livestock

Occupational

- Number of cultivators
- Workers
- Labors
- Marginal labors
- Off-farm labor

Climatic

- Rainfall (min to max)
- Temperature (min to max)

Geographic

- Area

In this construction of vulnerability index (VI), the method of Patnaik and Narayanan (2005) is used as follows:

$$VI = \left[ \sum_{i=1}^{n} (AI_i)^\alpha \right]^{1/\alpha} \Big/ n$$

..............................(3)

Where

       n= number of sources of vulnerability

α=n

AI= Average Index

**Data collection**

**Sources and Nature of data**

Data related to socio-economic characteristics of the household, disaster, and adaptation behavior for this study was primary in nature. The data was collected through a household survey as well as a key interview method in the watershed catchment areas of Sot Khola (Gadhi VDC, Lekhagaon VDC, and Kunathari VDC). As supplementary data and information, secondary data related to temperature, rainfall, and precipitation from 1990 to 2009 were collected from the Department of Hydrology and Meteorology (DHM) & the Government of Nepal (GON). The data set in this study is time-series data from 1980 to 2009 representing all parts of the country. Three climatic data variables: temperature, rainfall, and precipitation, which were recorded by the stations of Meteorology Departments all over the country, were different stations for temperature and rainfall records. These departments have main objectives to record temperature and rainfall for providing information and forecasting so that travel plans and agricultural production decisions can be done.

Temperature and rainfall data were recorded from nine stations: Taplejung, Biratnagar, Hetuda, Pokhara, Bhairahawa, Jomsom, Surkhet, Jumla, and Dhanghadi. The data covers 12 months (January to December).

**DATA ANALYSIS**

**METHOD OF DATA ANALYSIS**

**Method for Objective-1** was assessed by descriptive statistics and regression trend analysis mentioned in equation-1.

Let us fit the regression model to find a linear trend between the time series data(Y) and time (t) is given in the equation below.

$$y = a + b\,t \dots\dots\dots\dots\dots\dots(2)$$

Where

y = temperature or rainfall

t = time (year)

"a" and "b" are the parameters: intercept and coefficient of time respectively estimated by the principle of least squares.

## TOOLS OF DATA ANALYSIS

Data collected from secondary and primary sources were entered into the computer and converted into excel format. The data was processed by types and variables. Excel software was used for descriptive statistics of all data sets. The econometric method was used for analyzing data sets by using SPSS and STATA software packages. Statistical tools and relevant theoretical tools were employed to interpret the results. Then, the results were discussed.

# ANNEX III: PICTURES OF STUDY AREA (GADHI, LEKHAGAON, AND KUNATHARI)

## Pic 1: Lekhagaon VDC

Source: *Field Survey, 2015*

**Pic 2: Gadhi VDC**

*Source: Field Survey, 2015*

**Pic 3: Kunathari VDC**

Source: *Field Survey, 2015*

# ANNEX IX: PICTURES OF SOT KHOLA

**Pic  4: SotKhola, Kunathari**

Source: *Field Survey, 2015*

**Pic 5: SotKhola, Gadhi**

Source: *Field Survey, 2015*

**Pic 6: Sotkhola, Lekhagaon**

Source: *Field Survey, 2015*

# ANNEX X: PICTURES OF LANDSLIDES, DEPOSITION, AND SEDIMENTATION IN THE STUDY AREA

**Pic  7: Landslide in Gadhi**

Source: *Field Survey, 2015*

**Pic  8: Landslide in SotKhola**

Source: *Field Survey, 2015*

**Pic 9: Depostion and Sedimentation due to flood and landslide in SotKhola, Lekhgaon**

Source: *Field Survey, 2015*

**Pic 10: Bank Cutting, Deposition of Sedimentation in the Bank of Sot Khola**

Source: *Field Survey, 2015*

# ANNEX IV: PICTURES OF OBSERVATION, QUESTIONAIRE FILLING AND DISCUSSION

**Pic 11: Bank cutting, Deposition and Sedimentation in SotKhola flood 2014**

Source: *Field Survey, 2015*

**Pic  12: Landslides and Deposition of Sedimentation in road**

Source: *Field Survey, 2015*

**Pic 13: Displaced People in Rakshin and Damar, Kunathari in the flood of SotKhola, 2014**

Source: *Field Survey, 2015*

*Pic  14: Acclaimed land in which Sedimentation deposited by the flood of SotKhola, 2014*

Source: *Field Survey, 2015*